NO WAY HOME

No Way Home

The Crisis of Homelessness
and How to Fix It
with Intelligence and Humanity

KERRY JACKSON

CHRISTOPHER F. RUFO

JOSEPH TARTAKOVSKY

WAYNE WINEGARDEN

NEW YORK · LONDON

Contents

FOREWORD

STEPHEN MOORE

CALIFORNIA HAS A staggering homeless crisis that isn't being suffi-
ciently addressed by mayors or the politicians in Sacramento. In too
many instances, liberal policy designs are making the crisis worse.
This is harming the poor and making cities like San Francisco increas-
ingly unlivable.

Solutions that have worked in the past, as well as ideas that have
succeeded elsewhere, are needed to help the state cope with, and
ultimately improve, the declining conditions. It's with these objec-
tives in mind that the Pacific Research Institute had an on-the-ground
journey of discovery that ultimately shaped this book. The PRI team
visited shelters, listened to those who work with the homeless every
day, researched problems and solutions outside the state, and studied the methods of successful private organizations that are improving lives. PRI wanted to create a unique guide that state and local
policymakers, social service groups, academics, and grassroots organizations could draw from, and it did just that.

PRI has assembled a team of seasoned professionals, each of
whom drew on his area of expertise to contribute differing perspectives.

Christopher Rufo is a filmmaker, writer, and policy researcher. To
better understand the world of homelessness, Rufo walked the worst
streets on the West Coast, even spending a week on Los Angeles's
Skid Row. He's interviewed those who had been on the streets and
recovered, as well as the indirect victims of homelessness – residents
whose lives have been changed by the worsening homelessness
environments around them. His on-the-ground observations, not
from a statistical point of view but from a human point of view, were
critical to the project.

Joseph Tartakovsky, a former Gibson, Dunn & Crutcher litigator and
author of *The Lives of the Constitution: Ten Exceptional Minds That Shaped
America's Supreme Law*, provided a historical framework for *No Way
Home* that puts the phenomenon of homelessness into perspective.

Foreword

Tartakovsky's direct connection to homelessness today was sharpened by his participation in the *Martin v. City of Boise* case, in which two municipal ordinances that prohibited sleeping and camping in public spaces were challenged in court. The plaintiffs' win means that no city can arrest or ticket someone for camping in public unless that person has a publicly provided shelter available to them. In the course of litigating the case, Tartakovsky contacted dozens of cities, giving him a panoramic perspective and introducing him to an array of policies that otherwise might have remained hidden.

PRI senior fellow Wayne Winegarden brought his expertise as an economist to explore the effects of California's housing troubles on homelessness. Through his intensive background as a business economist, Winegarden tells the story of how public policy has exacerbated California's homelessness issues, from the steep cost of housing that's priced people out of homes to the unaffordable cost of living.

Kerry Jackson, an *Investor's Business Daily* editorial writer for 16 years and now PRI's fellow for California studies, has been researching and writing about homelessness and poverty in California for years. With this knowledge in hand, he was able to clearly outline the current state of homelessness.

Homelessness has become so disturbing that 95 percent of voters told the *Los Angeles Times* and the Los Angeles Business Council Institute that it is a serious or very serious problem, and it is in fact the top concern, beating out traffic and housing affordability. Across the state, likely voters also see homelessness as the Golden State's biggest problem, surpassing the economy and housing. Californians desperately want policymakers to make a difference.

But the solutions from the past have proven to be non-solutions that in many cases have made the homeless crisis worse, as it has gone from a mild nuisance (which many saw as someone else's problem) to one of the most pressing issues in the state. Now other cities outside of California, including Washington, D.C., Chicago, and Baltimore, are seeing a renewal of their homeless crisis.

The good news is the problem of homelessness can and should be solved. This book provides the roadmap to how to provide true and lasting help to the millions of homeless in America.

PREFACE

Cᴀʟɪꜰᴏʀɴɪᴀ's ʜᴏᴍᴇʟᴇꜱꜱ ᴄʀɪꜱɪꜱ is a tragedy. It is a tragedy for the homeless who bear the hardships and risks of living on the streets. It is a tragedy for the residents of California who are becoming accustomed to walking over human feces and sidestepping used needles on the sidewalk. It is a public health tragedy that enables medieval diseases such as typhus to incubate. And it is a tragedy for California's already tapped-out taxpayers who must pay the financial costs of it all.

The purpose of this book is to examine the causes of California's homelessness crisis, identify the missteps that worsen the problem, and offer policies to address the problem in the near and long term. The four coauthors at times come to different conclusions or suggest different policy emphases. Each author's perspective in this anthology is his own. Our understandings have been in part shaped by our backgrounds: Kerry Jackson is an independent journalist, opinion writer, and political analyst. He is currently a fellow with the Pacific Research Institute's Center for California Reform. Dr. Wayne Winegarden is a policy economist whose areas of study include the economic impacts from regulatory policies with an emphasis on their consequences on affordability and regressivity. Joseph Tartakovsky is a practicing attorney who has litigated and lectured on issues of homelessness and constitutional law and advised policymakers in California, Nevada, Oregon, and Washington on framing defensible policies and laws. Christopher F. Rufo is an activist, filmmaker, and policy analyst who covers poverty, homelessness, addiction, crime, and other afflictions. We felt that a joint approach would illuminate this thorny problem from multiple angles. Yet we all agree that ameliorating California's homelessness crisis is a policy priority of supreme urgency, for reasons of public order and safety, humanitarianism, and economic health.

Part I of the book is an overview of California's homelessness crisis. In the first chapter, Kerry Jackson documents the extent of the problem and its adverse consequences. Including rising crime, increased drug use, and the ever-growing threat to public health, this essay documents the ugly realities of California's homelessness problem.

Following up on this reporting, chapter 2, authored by Wayne

Winegarden, accounts for the high costs that Californians are bearing. These include the billions of dollars taxpayers spend managing and cleaning up after the crisis. But they also include the lost economic opportunities that are both visible (e.g., lost tourism and conference opportunities) and invisible (e.g., how the homeless problem encourages increased out-migration).

The final chapter of part I, authored by Joseph Tartakovsky, provides important background on how the legal response to homelessness has changed over time. As chapters 7 and 9 detail, the law is often an obstacle that makes addressing the homelessness crisis more difficult. This was not always the case. Tartakovsky reviews how the attitudes have swung from one extreme, treating homelessness as a crime, to the other, which enshrines homelessness as an uninfringeable right. Unwanted consequences arise from either extreme. As discussed in those later chapters, fixing the crisis requires that the law get the balance right.

Part II addresses why the homelessness crisis is magnitudes worse in California than anywhere else in the country. Jackson explores how state and local policies seem to actually incentivize homelessness in chapter 4.

In the fifth chapter, Christopher Rufo describes how people suffering from the perilous trifecta – the combination of mental illness, substance abuse, and homelessness – are an important component of California's homeless population. Sustainably solving California's homelessness crisis requires an understanding of the trifecta and the unique needs of this population.

Economic causes of homelessness matter too. The sixth chapter, by Winegarden, describes how a wide array of policies (from zoning regulations to climate change policies) have made California an unaffordable place to live. California's unaffordability increases people's financial vulnerability to black swan events. As a result, too many Californians who fall behind financially can never catch up and ultimately face a higher risk of becoming homeless.

Part II also tackles key policy trends making it more difficult to abate California's crisis. Chapter 7, authored by Tartakovsky, addresses the problems that arise from the changing interpretation of "quality of life" laws, typically ordinances addressing the day-to-day safety or livability of residents of communities. Changing interpretations at times encourage those experiencing homelessness to remain on the streets rather than to seek help, making it more difficult to help transition people from homelessness to permanent housing.

Beyond the growing legal impediments, it is fashionable to subscribe to a policy approach known as "housing first." Housing first is predicated on the belief that the most important initial step is to transition all homeless people into temporary, then permanent, homes. This approach is undoubtedly productive for some segments of the homeless population, but as Rufo explains in chapter 8, housing first policies can be counterproductive for the homeless population that suffers from mental illness and addiction. Transitioning certain individuals into permanent housing should begin with addressing their addictions or mental illnesses.

Tartakovsky explains in chapter 9 that judicial overreach – however well meaning – has recently become an obstacle. He describes why the legal decisions that create a constitutional right to live permanently on the street usurps legislative power and constrains state and local governments from implementing effective policies. This is especially problematic in an area of policymaking that requires maximum flexibility and accountability.

Leveraging the lessons learned from the earlier chapters, part III offers an overview of policy reforms that could sustainably address the homelessness problem.

Chapter 10, by Jackson and Winegarden, looks at what changemakers are doing to reduce homelessness and offers a catalog of solutions and recommendations learned from these real-life success stories. Included, as well, are Winegarden's suggestions for solving the affordability problems that plague California.

In the eleventh chapter, Tartakovsky recommends beneficial legal reforms or smarter policies. Rufo's chapter 12 discusses the benefits from a policy that combines strict enforcement of no-camping laws with the availability of the effective treatment programs.

Taken together, these policy reforms will help transition the current homeless population off the street, provide the necessary infrastructure to make this transition permanent, and address the underlying causes that push people into homelessness to begin with.

Kerry Jackson, editor

LIFE ON THE STREETS

Documenting California's Growing Homeless Crisis

POSTCARDS FROM THE EPICENTER

Just How Bad Is Homelessness in California?

KERRY JACKSON

CALIFORNIA HAS THE worst homelessness crisis in the country. The precise number of homeless Californians is hard to quantify. The US Department of Housing and Urban Development estimated that more than 151,000 were homeless in California in 2019, a 16 percent increase over the previous year.[1] Between 2016 and 2017, California's homeless population jumped 13.7 percent.[2]

The state has a disproportionate share of the nation's homeless population. While accounting for only 12 percent of the US total population, California accounts for 27 percent of all homeless people.[3] The portion of unsheltered homeless, at 71.7 percent, is nearly twice the national figure of 37.2 percent.[4]

Tragically, far too many of California's homeless are considered "chronically" homeless, that is, a person with a disabling condition who has been continuously homeless for one year or more. More than 39,000, or 40.6 percent, of the nation's more than 96,000 chronically homeless are located in California.[5] Of that number, 32,792, or 83.5 percent, are unsheltered. Only in Hawaii (85.8 percent) does a higher portion of the chronically homeless go unsheltered.[6]

Visitors to San Francisco sometimes don't know if what they're seeing on the streets is typical of the city or if they simply wandered into a bad part of town. In 2019, the estimated count was 17,595 homeless, a 30 percent increase from the previous year.[7] It "was by far," the *New York Times* reported, "the largest increase of the last eight years, according to the city's data."[8]

Following a decade of a stable homeless population that began in 2004, San Francisco's homeless population expanded by 17 percent between 2013 and 2017.[9]

In Southern California, the 2020 Greater Los Angeles Homeless Count found "66,436 people in Los Angeles County experiencing homelessness," the Los Angeles Homeless Services Authority reported.

"This represents a 12.7 percent rise from last year's point-in-time count. The city of Los Angeles saw a 14.2 percent rise to 41,290."[10]

The 2019 count found 58,936 homeless in the county, 36,300 in the city.[11] Over a six-year period, through roughly the end of 2017, "the number of those living in the streets and shelters of the city of L.A. and most of the county surged 75 percent – to roughly 55,000 from about 32,000," according to the *Los Angeles Times*.[12] In 2019, more than 1,000 homeless people died in Los Angeles County, an average of about three a day.

While the homeless populations are swelling in San Francisco and Los Angeles, the city of San Diego saw improvement in 2020. Its total fell to 4,887, a 4 percent decrease from the 5,082 counted in 2019.[13] The homeless count for San Diego County fell 6 percent in 2020, to 7,619.[14]

The homeless population in San Jose, the heart of Silicon Valley, has grown to more than 6,000 people, according to the most recent point-in-time (PIT) count in 2019. The 2017 count found 4,350 homeless individuals, whereas the 2015 count found a little more than 4,000, indicating a spike of roughly 50 percent over four years. Growing along with the totals has been the proportion of unsheltered homeless, a figure that has grown from 69 percent in 2015, to 74 percent in 2017, to 84 percent in 2019.[15]

Visitors to San Francisco sometimes don't know if what they're seeing on the streets is typical of the city or if they simply wandered into a bad part of town.

In Santa Clara County, the homeless population grew 31 percent from 2017 (7,394 individuals) to 2019 (9,706).[16]

In California's state capital, the county's homeless population has more than doubled since 2013. The *Sacramento Bee* reported in 2017 that there was "a daily fight for cleanliness and safety as homelessness surges" in the city's midtown section. The Midtown Association, funded by property owners, was "doubling down on its Clean and Safe program, in which workers walk the streets to scrub graffiti, pick up trash, clean up human waste, and help connect homeless people with social services and medical care."[17] Even then, before the doubling of the homeless count, there was a concern that the capital was becoming too much like San Francisco.[18]

Homelessness in California is not confined to its big cities. Suburbs and rural towns have also become "homes" to the homeless.

"California housing costs are spiraling so high that they are pushing the state's homelessness crisis into places it's never been before – sparsely populated rural counties," the *San Francisco Chronicle* reported in 2017. "A *Chronicle* analysis of biennial homeless counts taken early this year across California shows the sharpest increases occurred not in San Francisco and other urban centers but in out-of-the-way places such as the thickly forested Sierra Nevada and the dusty flatlands and low hills of the northern Sacramento Valley."[19]

In January 2020, Governor Gavin Newsom said homelessness "is now a dominant issue in rural California as well."[20] A month later, Sharon Rapport, director of California Policy for the Corporation for Supportive Housing, said, "We see homelessness in every part of our state. . . . It's not just in our urban centers, it's in our suburban areas, it's in our rural areas."[21]

The homeless population outside urban centers is difficult to pin down, particularly regarding the rural homeless. These populations tend to be more spread out, as shelters, soup kitchens, and other places where the homeless would gather are less centralized than they are in large cities.

The Cost of Homelessness

As this book documents in great detail, homelessness in California produces profound difficulties for both the homeless themselves and the communities they inhabit.

The homeless suffer from chronic and acute diseases, as well as threatening health conditions due to a lack of care and treatment from health professionals and family members. One study has determined that 85 percent of homeless individuals have chronic health conditions.[22] Disorders include cardiorespiratory diseases, tuberculosis, skin problems and infections, HIV/AIDS, bronchitis, pneumonia, nutritional deficiencies, and drug dependency. The homeless are also vulnerable to physical and sexual assault, experience sleep deprivation, and have higher mortality rates than the non-homeless.

Homelessness also puts the public at risk. This is particularly true in San Francisco, where the "streets are so filthy," reports National Public Radio, "that at least one infectious disease expert has compared the city to some of the dirtiest slums in the world."[23] One resident who lives in the South of Market neighborhood has documented an increase in methicillin-resistant *Staphylococcus aureus* on the streets of San Francisco.[24]

NBC Bay Area surveyed 153 blocks in downtown San Francisco and reported in February 2018:

> The Investigate Unit spent three days assessing conditions on the streets of downtown San Francisco and discovered trash on each of the 153 blocks surveyed. While some streets were littered with items as small as a candy wrapper, the vast majority of trash found included large heaps of garbage, food, and discarded junk. The investigation also found 100 drug needles and more than 300 piles of feces throughout downtown.[25]

Within that space were "popular tourist spots like Union Square and major hotel chains," as well as "City Hall, schools, playgrounds, and a police station."[26]

Complaints made to the city about the volumes of human waste in the streets have increased as the homeless population has risen. There were 1,748 complaints made in 2008. By 2017, they had grown to 21,000. Through October 2018, there were 20,400. Complaints of discarded needles have grown sharply as well.[27] Addressing these problems will not come cheaply. San Francisco mayor London Breed has proposed adding an additional $13 million to the city's current $65 million street-cleaning budget.[28]

The homeless also tend to be addicted to alcohol and various drugs and are often mentally ill. In chapter 5, Christopher Rufo notes that San Francisco, for instance, spends $370 million a year on mental health and substance abuse programs, many of which, he says, "cater to the city's homeless." He also reports that the city has passed a sweeping "mental health reform" that will increase spending by $500 million a year.

Rufo also documents the hundreds of millions spent on efforts to house the homeless. Still, the homeless remain, and the numbers show no sign of retreating.

California's reputation as a welcome dwelling place for the homeless has scared off prospective visitors. As Wayne Winegarden documents in chapter 2, a medical association based in Chicago announced in 2018 that it would no longer hold its convention in San Francisco after 2023 due to the "appalling street life."[29] A little more than a year later, Oracle, based in nearby Redwood City, said it was moving its OpenWorld conference to Las Vegas in 2020, where it would remain for

The homeless population in San Jose, the heart of Silicon Valley, has grown to more than 6,000 people, according to the most recent point-in-time (PIT) count in 2019.

at least three years. One reason given for the change was the steep cost of hotel rooms in the city, but the email sent to the San Francisco Travel Association also cited "poor street conditions."[30]

San Francisco Travel Association CEO Joe D'Alessandro told the *San Francisco Chronicle* that "33 percent of the 1,282 tourists questioned in a survey this year commissioned by the agency cited homelessness and dirty streets as the least attractive aspects of visiting the city."[31]

Access to public areas, such as sidewalks, parks, and streets, and public transportation has declined as the homeless take over more of these spaces with tents (which often conceal criminality), sleeping bags, and prone bodies. A Bay Area Rapid Transit patron survey found that ridership has declined in part due to "crime, cleanliness (or lack thereof) and homeless riders."[32] At the same time, homelessness is increasing the costs associated with criminal activity. Incarceration and property crimes committed to feed addictions are both public and private losses.

Part I of this book documents the homeless problem faced in communities across the Golden State today.

Winegarden puts a dollar figure on how growing homelessness is hurting individual taxpayers, business owners, and government. Because there is so much damage at so many levels, it is difficult to paint a full picture of the overall costs to the state in terms of public monies spent, business opportunities lost, the flight of human and financial capital, and lives disrupted and ruined. However, the data presented by Winegarden of the economic damage caused by California's homeless problem is sobering.

Joseph Tartakovsky, meanwhile, shows how public policy choices made over the years are fueling the state's out-of-control homelessness problem.

SQUANDERED OPPORTUNITIES

How Homelessness Hurts the Economy

2

WAYNE WINEGARDEN

THE SOCIAL COSTS of homelessness – including diseases, drugs, and violence – impose large and growing burdens on the homeless themselves, as well as the broader residents of California. The troubling economic consequences that result from these social costs – from lost economic opportunities to the costs of managing the crisis – are similarly intensifying.

Due to the wide differences in the types of economic costs, estimating one aggregate economic impact number is less meaningful than understanding the many ways that California's homelessness crisis undermines the economic well-being of all Californians. Consequently, instead of producing one macro cost number, this chapter documents the wide array of costs – quantifying these costs where possible – to demonstrate that sustainably addressing California's homelessness crisis is an important economic development priority in addition to a crucial social well-being priority.

Accounting for the Large Government Costs Created by the Homelessness Crisis

Perhaps the most visible economic costs from the homelessness crisis are reflected in government budgets. California's state and local governments are now spending billions of dollars annually trying to address the crisis and deal with its consequences.

Los Angeles, for instance, spent $619 million on homelessness in 2018. This includes the revenues that the city receives from Proposition HHH – a voter-approved initiative that provided $1.2 billion in bond revenues explicitly dedicated to addressing homelessness. Unfortunately, despite spending all of this money, the Los Angeles region by most measures is not making sufficient progress reining in its worst-in-the-country homelessness problem.[1]

A similar story is evident in San Francisco. In the 2019–2020 budget, the city allocated over $365 million, which is more than double the $157 million it dedicated to homelessness and supportive housing programs in its 2011–2012 budget.[2] San Francisco is spending this money on a comprehensive set of services that includes health care, outreach to the homeless, provisions for temporary shelters, and housing subsidies to help people remain in a private residence. Despite all of these programs and efforts, San Francisco's expenditures are, just as they are in Los Angeles, generally viewed as having been ineffective.

At the state level, California will spend nearly $1.2 billion in federal and state revenues addressing the state's homelessness crisis in the 2020–2021 budget year. Table 2.1 presents the intended allocation of these expenditures. Like the expenditures in Los Angeles and San Francisco, these cover a comprehensive set of health, outreach, housing support, and shelter services.

Instead of producing one macro cost number, this chapter documents the wide array of costs – quantifying these costs where possible – to demonstrate that sustainably addressing California's homelessness crisis is an important economic development priority in addition to a crucial social well-being priority.

For instance, California will spend tens of millions of dollars on its Rapid Rehousing program, which links recipients to community resources that identify housing opportunities for program clients, develops plans to prevent future housing instability, and provides financial assistance.[3] Other state programs spend tens of millions of dollars annually providing temporary shelter as well as the necessary social-support programs that the homeless population often requires.

In the latest attempt to address the problem, Governor Newsom announced (as of June 2020) a new approach called the Homekey program. It is the largest expenditure item that directly targets the homeless in the current state budget. This program uses federal COVID-19 support revenues to rehabilitate a variety of buildings (e.g., hotels, motels, vacant apartment buildings, and tiny homes) that can then be used to create housing options to serve people experiencing homelessness.[4] The Homekey program is derived from the Roomkey program

Table 2.1. 2020-2021 State Government Expenditures on Homeless Programs

GOVERNMENT PROGRAM/ DEPARTMENT	COST (MILLIONS)	NOTES
CARES Act – Coronavirus Relief Fund: Homekey	$550.0	*state/local governments*
Department of Housing and Community Development	$401.0	*federally funded programs for homelessness, local aid for homelessness, Homekey operating subsidies, various programs*
Office of Emergency Services	$6.6	*various homeless youth programs, youth emergency telephone network*
Department of Social Services	$179.3	*CalWORKS Homeless Assistance Program, Housing and Disability Advocacy Program*
Department of Health Care Services	$8.8	*Project for Assistance in the Transition from Homelessness*
University of California	$18.5	*basic needs funding – student hunger and homelessness programs, Rapid Rehousing*
California Community Colleges	$9.0	*Rapid Rehousing*
California State University	$6.5	*Rapid Rehousing*
California State Expenditures	**$1,179.7**	

Source: California State Budget Summary 2020–2021

that moved homeless people into empty hotels and motels during the COVID-19 pandemic.

Since California has the most dire homelessness crisis in the country, and it is so much worse compared to just a few years ago, the costs that state and local governments are now bearing dwarf the costs in other states as well as the historical costs that California has spent addressing the problem. Due to the significant increase in the costs of helping the homeless as of late, these additional costs represent lost opportunities for Californians – costs manifested in either a higher than necessary burden on taxpayers or the state underfunding other priorities (e.g., failing to adequately invest in California's highway and water systems) or both. While precisely defining these lost opportunities is difficult, what is certain is that opportunities *are lost* in order to pay for the increased costs created by the crisis.

The lost opportunities are even higher than the expenditures that are directly dedicated toward homelessness would indicate. California's state and local governments incur many other costs that are not documented under the housing and homeless programs budget line items. They are subsumed under the line items of other agencies and departments. As a 2017 report from the California state auditor noted, reviewing the City of Los Angeles's spending,

> although only four agencies and departments had budgetary allocations for homeless programs, at least 15 [agencies and departments] regularly engaged with homeless people, with some departments incurring large costs. For example, the report cited that the Los Angeles Police Department estimated it spent from $53.6 million to $87.3 million in one year on interactions with homeless people and the Bureau of Sanitation spent at least $547,000 in a year on cleanup of homeless encampments.[5]

Accounting for the adverse impacts on the budgets of other agencies significantly raises the annual budgetary cost from California's out-of-control homelessness problem.

A 2015 study from Santa Clara County, which details the crisis's impact on the budgets of other departments and agencies, provides some perspective regarding how large these costs can be.[6] In total, the report found that Santa Clara County spent $3.1 billion over six years, or an average of $520 million a year.[7] Of these expenditures,

> a total of $1.9 billion, or $312 million a year, was spent on health care. Valley Medical Center and its network of clinics spent $915 million on health care for homeless residents over six years, with another $387 million spent by private hospitals. The County Mental Health department spent $448 million,

County Drug and Alcohol Services spent $100 million, and $25 million was spent on emergency medical transportation.

Social welfare agencies including nonprofit service providers and county Social Services spent $463 million over six years. Justice system agencies spent $786 million over six years, or $196 million a year, most of it for jail costs.[8]

The Link between Rising Health Risks and Rising Economic Costs

The costs borne by public and private health care systems because of the homelessness crisis are one of the largest expenditures documented in the Santa Clara County report. These costs arise because homelessness is an important risk factor for many adverse health outcomes. In part due to these health risks, the unsheltered homeless population die, on average, 20 years earlier than people who are sheltered.[9] As noted by the California state auditor,

> The unsheltered homeless population also has an increased risk of exposure to communicable diseases. According to Public Health, as of February 2018, California was experiencing the largest person-to-person hepatitis A outbreak not related to a common source or a contaminated food product in the United States since the hepatitis A vaccine became available in 1996, and four counties had declared local outbreaks of the disease. The homeless populations in the CoC [continuum of care] areas for Los Angeles, San Diego, Santa Cruz, and Monterey counties, which have rates of unsheltered homelessness ranging between 60 percent and 80 percent, have been affected by these recent outbreaks. For example, according to minute orders approved by the San Diego County Board of Supervisors, from September 2017 through January 2018, San Diego County experienced a local health emergency caused by a hepatitis A outbreak in the homeless and illicit drug-using populations. Public Health reported that as of February 2018, 580 cases, 398 hospitalizations, and 20 deaths were associated with the hepatitis A outbreak in that county.[10]

The health risks are not limited to the homeless either. The potential outbreaks in the homeless community also create broader public health threats.[11] As *USA Today* documented,

> A hepatitis A outbreak occurred late last year in Los Angeles. The contagious illness can cause vomiting, nausea and jaundice. It has shown up on the West Coast and around the nation, including Kentucky, Utah and New Mexico, traced to the homeless and drug use.
>
> After cases of hepatitis A took off in Louisville in late 2017, the liver disease spread across Kentucky, sickening more than 4,000, about half of whom had to be hospitalized, and killing at least 43.[12]

While the above examples emphasize the risks from hepatitis A, California's infectious disease problem goes beyond any single disease. Shigella and other infectious diseases have been diagnosed in California's unsheltered homeless population and create health risks and large health costs for both the homeless and general populations. As an indication of how large these costs have become, many of these illnesses, like typhus, are commonly referred to as *medieval diseases* because they thrive in the unsanitary conditions that were prevalent long ago. As the unsanitary conditions on the streets of California now replicate those from the Middle Ages, the same adverse health outcomes are arising.

The Connection between Homelessness and Declining Business Opportunities

Beyond the health implications, the infamy of California's homelessness crisis is dimming the state's economic allure and contributing to lost economic opportunities. Business owners in Los Angeles, along San Francisco's famous Pier 39, and in San Francisco's Castro District have all complained that deteriorating conditions are discouraging tourism, reducing foot traffic, and costing their businesses revenue.[13] And it is not simply small businesses that are suffering. The city's homelessness crisis encouraged a major Chicago-based medical association "to move its $40 million convention out of San Francisco due to safety issues for its conventioneers."[14] These lost economic opportunities are not explicitly recorded anywhere, but they are no less real for the people who experience them.

Losses such as these, when coupled with the health and quality-of-life implications, also contribute to the disconcerting trend of businesses and families choosing to migrate to other states. As the California Department of Finance documented,

> California's population grew by 141,300 people between July 1, 2018 and July 1, 2019 to total 39.96 million, according to official population estimates released today by the Department of Finance. *This represented a growth rate of 0.35 percent which was a further decline from our last official estimate. Our previous estimates were the lowest since 1905* when [the Demographic Reporting Unit's] annual population estimates begin and the trend continued. The state's population growth rate had been below 1 percent since 2005. The reasons for the decline during this decade were, by order of magnitude, higher domestic out-migration, lower immigration to California, and fewer births.[15]

The state's population growth is stagnating because more Californians are choosing to move to other states than residents from other states are choosing to move to California. Although this migration away from California is a long-term problem, unique attributes to the current out-migration connect to the growing homeless problem. These differences are visualized in figure 2.1.

Figure 2.1 measures the migration of Californians based on the IRS Statistics of Income (SOI) data, so it is a measure of households who file taxes.[16] The bars in figure 2.1 present the net migration of filing households (households moving to California from other states minus households moving from California to other states) relative to the number of Californians who did not migrate during the year. Except for 2001 and 2012, more tax-filing households moved

Business owners in Los Angeles, along San Francisco's famous Pier 39, and in San Francisco's Castro District have all complained that deteriorating conditions are discouraging tourism, reducing foot traffic, and costing their businesses revenue.

out of California from year to year than moved into the state. However, prior to the current period, there was a strong relationship between economic growth and migration to California.

California's economy is more volatile than the national average – it booms stronger during good times and crashes harder during bad times. The impact from this volatility can be seen in the net migration numbers: the number of households migrating away from California moderates during economic expansions but accelerates during the periods of economic stagnation.

This relationship has broken down since the 2008–2009 recession. Despite the economic recovery, the migration of tax-filing households accelerated during the current economic expansion, which contrasts sharply with the other periods. The growing exodus is consistent with declines in the quality of life in California, which includes the state's homelessness problem.

The exodus of Californians diminishes the state's economic vibrancy. Therefore, stemming this tide should be a top economic development priority for California. Among the many policy changes necessary to curb the relocations, addressing the homelessness crisis is one of them.

Figure 2.1. California Net Migration Trends

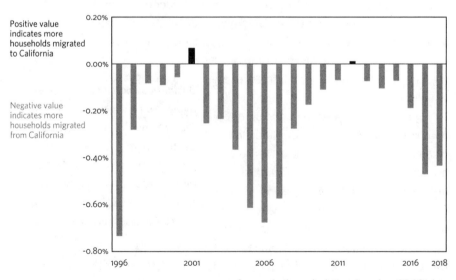

Source: Author calculations based on IRS SOI data

The High Cost of Ending Homelessness in California

The large and varied costs created by the homeless crisis demonstrates that the state bears billions of dollars in costs each and every year. Compounding these costs, the current expenditures are merely managing the symptoms of the problem, but they are not sustainably addressing its causes. As other chapters detail, the causes are complex. But, as I document in chapter 6, the declining affordability of the state is a significant component. Ironically, the same policies that make California unaffordable and help fuel homelessness are also inflating the costs that Californians must pay to fix it.

To get a sense of the enormity of the expenditures required to "end homelessness," a 2019 study by the Bay Area Economic Institute estimated the "scale of the resources necessary to end homelessness [in the Bay Area] under current methods of building and providing services."[17] The institute's calculation estimates

> that $12.7 billion would be required to create a new unit of permanent housing (at $450,000 per unit) for each of the 28,200 people experiencing homelessness identified in PIT [point-in-time] counts. Providing services (at $25,000 per person per year) to half of that population over 10 years would require an additional $3.5 billion.[18]

With some adjustments described below, table 2.2 leverages the Bay Area Economic Institute's methodology to provide an estimate for the costs of ending homelessness across the entire state. The first adjustment assumes two scenarios regarding the number of affordable homes required to address the problem. A low-end scenario assumes that the number of new affordable housing units required is equal to one-half of the Californians that the Department of Housing and Urban Development (HUD) identified as homeless in 2019. The high-end scenario uses the Bay Area Economic Institute's assumption, which is that a new affordable housing unit is required for each person identified as homeless, according to the 2019 HUD PIT count.

The second adjustment changes the cost to build affordable housing to reflect the average cost in California rather than in the Bay Area only. The cost to build an affordable housing unit in California is based on the estimates from the Terner Center for Housing Innovation at the University of California, Berkeley.[19] According to the Terner Center,

> the cost of building a 100-unit affordable project in California increased from $265,000 per unit in 2000 to almost $425,000 in 2016. The same trends that increase costs for market-rate housing (such as land pricing, construction costs, and regulation) impact affordable housing. In addition, affordable projects are often subject to increased local scrutiny, further inflating costs. A 2014 study found that local government design requirements for affordable housing added an average of 7 percent in total costs, and that community opposition (measured by holding four or more community meetings) increased expenses by 5 percent.[20]

The estimated $425,000 needed to build a unit of affordable housing is arguably the most important factor driving up the costs of enabling permanent housing solutions for the current homeless population. And these costs are the average across the state. They are much higher in specific high-cost localities. For instance, according to a 2019 *USA Today* report, the cost to build affordable housing in Los Angeles was nearly $700,000 per unit. This means that the estimated cost to construct affordable housing in Los Angeles is actually higher than the county's median sales price for a home, which was $618,000.[21] This comparison alone demonstrates why, under the current policy environment, sustainably addressing the homelessness crisis imposes such a high economic cost on the state and why waiving or (ideally) repealing these costs are necessary reforms for addressing the homeless crisis.

With respect to the costs for providing the necessary support services, table 2.2 adopts the estimated cost from the Bay Area Economic Institute that, on average, one-half of the homeless population will require $25,000 per year of services over a 10-year period. Since these costs will be incurred over time, the costs incurred in the future need to be discounted into today's dollars. Table 2.2 estimates the present value of these expenditures based on a 2 percent discount rate, which is approximately the interest rate that the State of California pays on its debt.[22]

Table 2.2. Costs to End Homeless in California

	LOW-END	HIGH-END
Homeless Count	75,639	151,278
Cost to Build Affordable Housing	$425,000	$425,000
Cost to House Current Homeless Population (billions)	*$32.1*	*$64.3*
Per-person service cost per year	$25,000	$25,000
Aggregate service cost per year for one-half of the population (billions)	$1.9	$1.9
Present Value Aggregate service cost over 10 years (billions)	$17.0	$17.0
Cost to End Homelessness over 10 Years (billions)	*$49.1*	*$81.3*

Source: Author calculations based on Bay Area Economic Institute methodology and data from HUD and Terner Center for Housing Innovation at UC Berkeley

Based on these data and assumptions, the cost to build sufficient affordable housing and the present value of providing the requisite support services ranges between $49.1 billion and $81.3 billion, or between 1.6 percent and 2.6 percent of the total size of California's economy in 2019. And these estimates could even be low. According to the National Alliance to End Homelessness, a chronically homeless person costs the taxpayer $35,578 a year rather than the $25,000 estimate used in table 2.2.[23] Based on this higher figure, the present value of the costs would range between $56.3 billion and $88.5 billion or between 1.8 percent and 2.8 percent of the state's economy.

These calculations demonstrate that resolving the homelessness crisis is intolerably expensive in California because the idea of affordable housing in the state is nearly an oxymoron. Since government policies have inflated costs so excessively, addressing the homeless problem requires tens of billions of dollars that cannot be justified based on the physical costs alone.

The exorbitant costs of building affordable housing in California paint a bleak picture. Not only are Californians bearing high costs from the crisis, but they must also pay an exceptionally large price to mitigate the crisis. This large price diminishes the effectiveness of the state and local governments as they attempt to sustainably address the problem.

Part I: Life on the Streets

Yet there are reasons to be optimistic. The excessive costs of building affordable houses are driven by the government's economic and land-use policies (both state and local). Since law and government policies are inflating the costs, changing these policies can significantly lessen the cost to build and maintain affordable housing.

These calculations demonstrate that resolving the homelessness crisis is intolerably expensive in California because the idea of affordable housing in the state is nearly an oxymoron. Since government policies have inflated costs so excessively, addressing the homeless problem requires tens of billions of dollars that cannot be justified based on the physical costs alone.

As a result, sustainably addressing the problem *can* be made more affordable. There are additional benefits from these policy reforms. By eliminating the policies that help make housing unaffordable in California, the policy reforms will reduce the economic pressures that drive many people into homelessness in the first place. These reforms will be discussed in more detail in chapter 10.

FROM VAGRANCY TO HOMELESS RIGHTS

A Brief History of the "Law" of Homelessness

3

Joseph Tartakovsky

HOMELESSNESS WAS ALREADY part of American life – and therefore American law – before George Washington's great-grandfather even set foot on our free shores.[1] So it will remain, as long as we have more humans than homes; as long as mental illness remains incurable, economies slump, and drugs addict; and as long as bad choices, worse luck, infirmity, wanderlust, and rebellion remain part of the human condition.

The law in this country has long recognized that the causes of homelessness are as varied as human nature itself. It was during the Civil War era, for instance, that the word "homeless" first entered our legal lexicon. Lawsuits from that period show Americans stranded without an abode through financial distress, or by the loss of a caretaker, or because of physical or mental disability.[2]

What has changed – dramatically so – has been the *character* of the laws that regulate homelessness, or, more specifically, the conduct associated with that condition of life. We should be proud of the general trend, which has been to replace castigation and contempt with sympathy and support. Today, the old models of punitive workhouses and drafty police station "tramp rooms" are memories of an unfeeling past. They have been replaced by "wraparound" service shelters with professional staffs trained in medicine or social work.[3]

For most of our history, the only publicly funded service offered by most communities was having the policeman show a homeless man the city limits. Today we spend billions to help the homeless. In 2019, Los Angeles spent an average of $1.7 million a day directly on homelessness.[4] Americans may dispute whether there is a "right" to be homeless, but today they agree that it is certainly not a *crime*. The famed professor and social critic William Graham Sumner (1840–1910) once said that the "drunkard in the gutter is just where he ought to be." We do not talk this way anymore. But more to the point: we do not *think* this way either.

The unavoidable task for society, rather, is to strike a balance between the rights of the unhoused and the rights of everyone else. At times those rights will clash. What this amounts to, in legal terms, is that homeless individuals must be treated humanely – as human beings, with the same set of constitutional rights as anyone else – but also that communities must have the power to regulate certain forms of antisocial conduct, whether committed by the homeless or by anyone else.

The Era of Exclusionary Laws

America has always had a "homeless" class. In 1640s Boston, over 100 years before the Revolution, "vagrant persons" were among the categories of outcasts that peace officers were charged with apprehending. A century later, and still well before the founding, the "wandering poor" or "study beggars" trod backcountry roads or massed in bustling seaport towns such as Philadelphia or Baltimore.[5] A New York City newspaper in 1734 was already lamenting that "beggarly people wander about the streets" – and urged construction of public buildings to jail them.[6]

After the Civil War there emerged in America the despised invader known as the "tramp" or "bum" – rendered newly mobile by continent-spanning railroads.[7] Ministers reiterated their old warning that soup kitchens attracted idlers from afar.[8] Well into the early twentieth century Americans cast opprobrium on "drifters," "loafers," "Okies," and "hobos." The laws that Americans passed in reaction reflected the ill will toward the people so labeled. In fact, Americans long strove to legislate homelessness out of existence, or at least out of sight.

At the founding, the condition of living semipermanently on the streets was, on paper at least, outlawed. A Washington, D.C., law from 1804, typical of its kind, prescribed hard labor for anyone within an expansive list of undesirable categories, among them "vagrants," "idle or disorderly persons," persons who "have no visible means of support, or are likely to become chargeable to the City as paupers," people "who can show no reasonable cause of business or employment in the City," people "who have no fixed place of residence" or "cannot give a good account of themselves," or "night walkers."[9]

In this era, safety nets, thin as could be, came in the form of family, friends, and churches. The law reflected the consensus that the homeless were not to be supported at the public expense. In 1837, the US Supreme Court upheld a law from New York State that required ship captains, if they carried to port a person with "no legal settlement," to pledge to reimburse New York City for the cost of any passengers who became a public charge within three years of arrival. The message: Do not give us your tired, your hungry, your huddled masses yearning to breathe free – unless they can find a way to support themselves in fairly short order.[10]

US Supreme Court justice Philip Pendleton Barbour wrote that it was as "necessary" for a state to take "precautionary measures against the moral pestilence of paupers" as to "guard against the physical pestilence."[11] Often the determination to keep people out was sharpened by racial animosity. The ugly California Constitution of 1879 had a special section empowering authorities to go after "vagrants, paupers, mendicants" – if they were Chinese.[12]

By the mid-twentieth century, the most overt exclusionary laws were being repealed or struck down by courts. This reflected a softening of popular attitudes. For instance, in 1941, the US Supreme Court decided *Edwards v. California*, a challenge to California's "anti-Okie" law. A man named Fred Edwards was sentenced to six months in jail for "bringing into the State [an] indigent person who is not a resident of the State" – in that case, his penniless, jobless brother-in-law from Texas.[13] California defended the law on the not unreasonable ground that, since 1933, some 350,000 people had flooded into the Golden State and imposed staggering new strains on California's welfare budgets.[14] (During the winter of 1935–1936, California and Florida set up border patrols to blockade indigents from entering.)[15]

Homelessness was already part of American life – and therefore American law – before George Washington's great-grandfather even set foot on our free shores. So it will remain, as long as we have more humans than homes; as long as mental illness remains incurable, economies slump, and drugs addict; and as long as bad choices, worse luck, infirmity, wanderlust, and rebellion remain part of the human condition.

The court found that California lacked power to enforce such a law, because that law encroached on federal authority to regulate "commerce" among the states. But the justices, revealing their less legalistic views, added that Americans, in their view, had entered a new era of solicitude for the plight of the unfortunate. "[T]he theory of the Elizabethan poor laws," they wrote, "no longer fits the facts."[16] The justices – all but one appointed by President Franklin Delano Roosevelt – condemned the old 1837 decision that left New York City's ship captains on the hook. "Whatever may have been the notion then prevailing," the court wrote, "[p]overty and immorality are not synonymous."[17]

The Fall of "Vagrancy" or "Loitering" Laws

As laws of outright exclusion fell, the chief legal weapon used against the homeless was "vagrancy" laws. These were mostly archaic hold-overs – derived, at some level, from the English poor laws and their attempt, as feudalism frayed, to control roaming laborers or runaway serfs.[18] American vagrancy laws took the form of sweeping prohibitions against broad categories of conduct or character. For instance, the California Penal Code provided that "[e]very idle, or lewd, or dissolute person, or associate of known thieves" was declared a "vagrant" and punishable by fine or imprisonment. A California judge construed "dissolute" to mean anyone "loosed from restraint, unashamed, lawless, loose in morals and conduct." This definition was enough to snare everyone from petty criminals to obnoxious political speechmakers.[19]

In the late 1940s and early 1950s, the US Supreme Court came to express its distaste for these dragnet laws. Some justices claimed to see "serious constitutional questions" about the validity of California's anti-vagrancy statute.[20] They disliked how a California judge told jurors that a defendant could be punished not for committing any particular misdeed but for being a person of "a certain status." "Vagrancy," that judge said, "is a status or a condition and it is not an act."[21]

Then in 1965, the US Supreme Court, in a case out of Birmingham, Alabama, disapproved of a law that forbade a person to "stand" or "loiter" in ways obstructing the sidewalk, since, in practice, the law meant that "a person may stand on a public sidewalk in Birmingham only at the whim of any police officer of that city."[22] Justice Abe Fortas wrote, mockingly, that if the statute were literally applied, the "use of the sidewalks" by citizens "would be hazardous beyond measure." What was really going on, he continued, was that the defendant, Albert Shuttlesworth, was a Black civil rights activist leading a boycott at the time of arrest.[23] The court did not reach the constitutional issue, but the decision captured the trend already in motion in courts across the nation: the Constitution, particularly its due process clause in the Fourteenth Amendment, would be read to prohibit laws that gave limitless discretion to police officers.

The US Supreme Court put the nail in the coffin of vagrancy laws – as many state courts and lower federal courts had already been doing for years – in *Papachristou v. City of Jacksonville* (1972). Jacksonville's vagrancy law had been used to arrest everyone from multiracial revelers driving to a nightclub to Black men seen pacing by wary store owners or a body-shop worker "reputed to be a thief."[24] The law was in essence a variation of the founding-era vagrancy laws. Jacksonville's ordinance authorized the punishment of "vagrants," defined impressively as

> [r]ogues and vagabonds, or dissolute persons who go about begging, common gamblers, persons who use juggling or unlawful games or plays, common drunkards, common night walkers, thieves, pilferers or pickpockets, traders in stolen property, lewd, wanton and lascivious persons, keepers of gambling places, common railers and brawlers, persons wandering or strolling around from place to place without any lawful purpose or object, habitual loafers, disorderly persons, persons neglecting all lawful business and habitually spending their time by frequenting houses of ill fame, gaming houses, or places where alcoholic beverages are sold or served, persons able to work but habitually living upon the earnings of their wives or minor children.[25]

The court found laws like this nothing more than "nets making easy the roundup of so-called undesirables."[26] It gave cover to officers for racially motivated detentions. It also countenanced irrational results: the police could arrest a man for walking at night even though he did so "hopeful that sleep-inducing relaxation will result." Or the law could punish the poor man living on a spouse's salary while seeking work yet leave alone "unemployed pillars of the community who have married rich wives."[27] The court found the law unconstitutionally "vague" under the due process clause of the Fourteenth Amendment because it "fails to give a person of ordinary intelligence fair notice that his contemplated conduct is forbidden by the statute" and "encourages arbitrary and erratic arrests and convictions."[28]

The unavoidable task for society, rather, is to strike a balance between the rights of the unhoused and the rights of everyone else.

Another form of law traditionally wielded against homeless individuals – the laws against "loitering" that are a close cousin of vagrancy laws – continued to fall as well. In 1983, the US Supreme Court struck down a California statute that required those who "loiter" or "wander" on the streets to provide a "credible and reliable" identification and to "account" for their "presence" when requested by a peace officer.[29] Edward Lawson was a dreadlocked, eloquent Black man who had been detained or arrested 15 times in two years while traversing Los Angeles. Whether he or any other person provided a "credible and reliable" answer was entirely in the officer's discretion. The court found that this law, like Jacksonville's vagrancy law, "furnishes a convenient tool for harsh and discriminatory enforcement by local prosecuting officials, against particular groups deemed to merit their displeasure."[30]

The cases above involved suspected racial or political targeting. But the lesson to lawmakers was broader: draft with precision, specifying *exactly* what problematic conduct is prohibited. This alone can (1) give the public fair notice of what to avoid and (2) confine the discretion available to officers, so that the conduct is prohibited on equal terms and consistently enforced.

* * *

But as will be shown below, though homelessness may always have been with us, it has never been so visible and so central a civic issue in so many cities.

PART II

HOW CALIFORNIA BECAME FIRST IN HOMELESSNESS

Decades of Bad Policy and Legal Decisions

INCENTIVIZING HOMELESSNESS

How Local and State Policies Encourage Homelessness

4

KERRY JACKSON

CALIFORNIA MAKES UP only 12 percent of the US population, yet the state is "home" to between 25 and 30 percent of the country's homeless population. How can this be? Are the homeless drawn to this state? Or do conditions exist that reward the poor decisions that can lead to homelessness? These possibilities can't be dismissed as easily as some policymakers and homeless activists-advocates want them to be.

When state and local governments increase their relative generosity, they encourage the homeless to move to California from other regions. According to Jennifer Amanda Jones, a professor who studies nonprofits, "problems migrate." "Almost 40 percent of San Francisco's homeless population became homeless in a city other than San Francisco," Jones writes in *Nonprofit Quarterly*. "Most (24 percent) hail from California, but many (15 percent) from around the United States."[1]

The chapters in this section explore the causes of California's growing homelessness, from public policies that appear to actually incentivize homelessness to a worsening state housing crisis that puts housing out of reach for too many. The chapters also explore "quality-of-life" laws that can improve circumstances or undermine them, "housing first" policies that turn a blind eye to alcoholism and drug abuse among the homeless, and misguided court rulings that make it tough for policymakers to combat a worsening problem.

Public Policies

San Francisco today is known as a city that is welcoming to the homeless. The *San Francisco Chronicle*, for instance, has acknowledged a "perception" that the city is a refuge for those who refuse to enter programs that would get them off the streets. That view is based in part on the city's reputation in recent years for refusing to enforce laws as forcefully and consistently as it should against trespassing, aggressive panhandling, tent encampments, blocking sidewalks, and defecating and urinating in public places.[2]

With the election of Chesa Boudin as San Francisco district attorney, it has in fact become official policy to allow selected criminal behavior to go unpunished. Boudin ran on the promise that he wouldn't prosecute quality-of-life crimes, such as "public camping, offering or soliciting sex, public urination, blocking a sidewalk, etc.,"[3] all of which, except for the possible exception of offering or soliciting sex, are inherent to homelessness. If Boudin "is able to implement his policy vision" – which includes a $1.5 million fund to pay for auto glass repair in a city where automobile break-ins are rampant – writes Christopher Rufo in chapter 5, the homeless "numbers would increase, perhaps dramatically."

California has made life, in a sense, comfortable for the homeless by opposing mandatory treatment for mental illness and drug addiction as a condition for housing, loose "policing of street activities," and generous benefits.

San Francisco also "seems" to have "normalized" assault, "at least when committed by the homeless," Manhattan Institute fellow Heather Mac Donald has reported. She quotes a resident who says, "anyone who has lived in San Francisco for five years has either been attacked by a homeless person or has a friend who has been attacked." But the attacks are no longer mentioned at public hearings "since doing so brings on accusations that they are criminalizing homelessness."[4] The homeless are apparently fed to the point of contentment, tap into free wireless networks, and can charge their devices, which Mac Donald says are used to barter goods, in public facilities.

California has made life, in a sense, comfortable for the homeless by opposing mandatory treatment for mental illness and drug addiction as a condition for housing,[5] loose "policing of street activities,"[6] and generous benefits, which Rufo will explore in chapter 8 when he discusses the Housing First program.[7] San Francisco – which has been receiving "an influx of about 450 chronically homeless people a year," says the *San Francisco Chronicle* – is, for instance, thought of as a "sanctuary" city "for people who are unwilling to participate in programs designed to get them off, and keep them off, a life in the streets." By the Bay, they have "the option to flout the law with impunity."[8]

"San Francisco has the ideal policy conditions to sleep on the streets, feed an addiction, and commit property crimes to survive – with little or no enforcement from the state," Rufo notes. In Mac Donald's words, "the city enables the entire homeless lifestyle."[9] She found one 50-year-old homeless man who told her "San Francisco is the place to go if you live on the streets. There are more resources – showers, yeah, and housing." A 31-year-old who "arrived in San Francisco from Martinez, northeast of the city, four years ago, trailing a long criminal record," also "came for the benefits."[10]

It's not unusual for the homeless to be treated in ways that makes them contented in their state of need. As Wayne Winegarden notes in chapter 2, when the coronavirus pandemic arrived in 2020, San Francisco placed about 1,200 homeless people in city hotels under California governor Gavin Newsom's Project Roomkey.[11] The city provided these quarantined homeless with alcohol, tobacco, medical cannabis, and other substances "in an effort to prevent a handful," the *San Francisco Chronicle* reported, "from going outside to get the substances themselves."[12]

The provision of these substances is part of the city's "harm reduction" effort, which in theory "promotes methods of reducing the physical, social, emotional, and economic harms associated with drug and alcohol use and other harmful behaviors on individuals and their community. Harm reduction methods and treatment goals are free of judgment or blame and directly involve the client in setting their own goals."[13]

Not everyone is persuaded that it works. In fact, the policy could be a contributor to the homelessness problem. Journalist and San Francisco resident Erica Sandberg has seen more harm "production" than "reduction":

Visit city neighborhoods ranging from the iconic Union Square and the Financial District to historically troubled areas such as the Tenderloin, Civic Center, and South of Market, and the unintended consequences of harm reduction become hard to ignore. The advocates have certainly succeeded in reducing stigma - it's easy to find people openly injecting into their arms, legs, toes, and necks. Their exposed flesh shows infected sores; they stumble, fall, and pass out. There seem to be more of them, and in worse condition, every day. Addicts congregate on sidewalks, in parks, subway stations, and outside businesses. They die in school doorways.[14]

Regarding the harm reduction objective of Project Roomkey, Sandberg says the combination "ensures the protection of neither the homeless hotel guests nor the general public."[15]

Homeless "Advocates"

Too often, policies are shaped by those who say they are advocates for the homeless, but in reality, they are working against them. What might be loosely called a "homeless-industrial complex" protects those on the streets as if they are an endangered species. The sidewalks and tent cities are their natural habitats, from which they cannot be removed.[16] Many self-labeled "advocates," excluding the countless people who have honorably committed their lives to minimizing the suffering of those on the streets, are less interested in ending homelessness than perpetuating it. As noted by Rufo, there are some who believe "the homeless have a 'human right' to languish in the streets." In fact, even "suggesting that some of the homeless are making a choice is heresy in official circles," says Mac Donald.[17]

In some cases, this thinking is institutionalized for self-seeking reasons.

It's not unusual for the homeless to be treated in ways that makes them contented in their state of need.

"I do not know of any community plan that actually details how to dismantle the existing homeless service system after homelessness has ended," Joel John Roberts writes in *Poverty Insights*. "Where do all of the executive directors, development directors, and finance directors go after the agencies go out of business? How about the social workers, security guards, and peer counselors? Do we sell off all the agencies' property and assets?"[18]

Charitable groups, he continues, "trend toward perpetuation rather than elimination." When local homeless agencies close their doors, it's "not because homelessness has ended, but because they financially cannot keep their doors open." Roberts also suggests that "conscience laundering" plays a part in the maintenance of the homelessness status quo.[19]

"Is all of this charitable energy to end homelessness simply a guilt-relieving exercise for those of us who are not homeless?" he asks.[20]

A *Huffington Post* contributor who identifies herself as a former homeless activist from Seattle says, "When I tell you that there is a homeless-industrial complex problem in Seattle, I'm speaking from experience."[21] Kenneth Alpern, a Southern California physician, has seen activists who "are absolutely OK with creating, promoting, and indefinitely extending the homeless crisis to create another governmental bureaucracy with no motivation to fix the problem of mental illness, drug abuse, and a new generation of forgotten souls."[22] Edward Ring of the California Policy Center warns that "a homeless-industrial complex has arisen in California that acquires power and profit by pursuing an utterly dysfunctional strategy" and "has grown into a voracious leviathan, devouring billions in taxpayers' money."[23] He adds,

> And for all practical purposes, and with all that money, they have just made the problem worse. This is because you can't ensure the rule of law when you permit people to wander the streets stoned out of their minds, or sprawled across park benches in a heroin stupor, or drinking and carousing all night long, urinating and defecating everywhere, and then permit them to receive free food and bedding in a shelter two blocks from the beach with no curfew and no restrictions on behavior. But that's what they did in Venice Beach.

In San Francisco, the Coalition on Homelessness, says Sandberg, "opposes any intervention in homeless issues unless it will 'provide housing and services.' . . . Coalition members attend meetings, protest so-called sweeps (cleaning out encampments), and verbally abuse anyone who doesn't want massive shelters that function as havens for drug use and criminal activity to be built next to their residences."[24]

Not every charitable group or activist organization that works with the homeless hopes to perpetuate homelessness for self-seeking reasons. As Roberts notes, "Within the homeless services and housing world, the goal of ending homelessness in this country is a public expression that the homeless charity world truly wants to go out of business."[25] But there are enough influential groups, as well as bureaucracies, which seek their own immortality, enabling the homeless rather than genuinely trying to lift them off the streets and back into mainstream life.

HOMELESS, ADDICTED, AND INSANE

The "Perilous Trifecta" Puts
San Francisco's Policy Regime to the Test

5

CHRISTOPHER F. RUFO

SAN FRANCISCO is coming undone. In recent years, the city has manifested a series of visible and persistent inequalities, with a spoils-to-the-victor world for its technological elite and a chaotic, brutalized world for its dispossessed. There are thousands of new millionaires in the city, and, by the latest estimates, 18,000 people in and out of homelessness.[1] While the traditional Anglo-American instinct in the face of inequality is to politely ignore it, San Francisco is tightly bound by its geography, so there is no place to hide. The headquarters of Uber, Twitter, and Square are blocks away from the open-air drug markets of the Tenderloin, Mid-Market, and SoMa; the city's old families going to the San Francisco Opera have to cross through the tent encampments of the Civic Center.

Residents, property owners, and small businesses – which pay an enormous premium to live and work in San Francisco – have begun to erupt in frustration. Citizens tell pollsters that homelessness is the city's most pressing issue and business owners tell survey-takers that "conditions on [the] streets have progressively deteriorated."[2] In short, the cruel dichotomy – globalized prosperity and localized depravity – cannot be ignored any longer.

The city, for its part, has begun coming to terms with the crisis. Mayor London Breed hired a director of mental health reform, Dr. Anton Nigusse Bland, who quickly compiled a statistical summary of the problem. People have long known that San Francisco has a homelessness crisis, but Nigusse Bland discovered a population-within-a-population – the so-called perilous trifecta – that has left city leaders aghast. The data sheet on the perilous trifecta is nothing short of catastrophic: there are 4,000 men and women in San Francisco who are simultaneously homeless, psychotic, and addicted to alcohol, meth, and heroin; 70 percent have been on the streets for more than 5 years; 40 percent have been on the streets for more than 13 years.[3]

This is the city's fundamental predicament. How do you help people in the grips of the perilous trifecta? What interventions could make progress? Where do city officials even start? It's almost impossible to understate the depths of this challenge. If social scientists wanted to design a population for a laboratory experiment on modern pathologies, it would look much like the perilous trifecta. In the past year, the city has released a furious stream of task force reports and demands for action, but underneath this patina of confidence lies a feeling that San Francisco is slouching toward dystopia and that people are scrambling to find a solution.

Everyone – from the ascendant progressive-socialists to the remnants of the law-and-order coalition – seems to recognize that the status quo is untenable. San Francisco's current policy toward the perilous trifecta can be best described as compassionate neglect. Every year, the chronically homeless cycle through the institutions of the socialized state, from hospitals, jails, and shelters to sobering centers, case management appointments, and 72-hour psychiatric holds. The local government provides enough to meet an outward standard of compassion but not enough to alter the trajectories of the homeless. The result is a disaster, which has drawn criticism across the political spectrum, with progressives demanding more funding for existing programs, and moderates bewildered by the eternal recurrence of tents, needles, and feces in their neighborhoods.

The current policy regime can be divided into three domains – the hospital, the jail, and the subsidized apartment. Together, these institutions represent the new orthodoxy of the socialized state: they reduce homelessness to a set of social-scientific variables, to be manipulated through the intensive application of the medical and social sciences.

As part of its medical system, San Francisco currently spends more than $370 million per year on mental health and substance abuse programs, many of which cater to the city's homeless. In a recent audit of the behavioral health system, the city's budget and legislative analyst found that 70 percent of all psychiatric emergency visits involved a homeless individual and that 66 percent of all visitors had co-occurring mental health and substance abuse disorders.[4] In total, the top 5 percent of "super-users," the majority of whom fall into the perilous trifecta, accounted for 52 percent of total systemwide service use. Doctors at San Francisco General see the same set of patients so frequently, they have developed an entire vocabulary to describe the population that circles in and out of their doors.[5]

Every year, the chronically homeless cycle through the institutions of the socialized state, from hospitals, jails, and shelters to sobering centers, case management appointments, and 72-hour psychiatric holds.

The carceral system is next. According to the San Francisco County Jail, the homeless account for 40 percent of all inmates – despite being less than 1 percent of the city's overall population, and despite the fact that San Francisco has rapidly decriminalized many quality-of-life crimes associated with homelessness.[6] Again, the perilous trifecta looms large. Inmates with co-occurring mental health and substance abuse disorders are more likely to be homeless and more likely to be charged with a violent crime compared to the general jail population.[7] The pithy observation about deinstitutionalization is largely true: the people who might have once lived in the state mental hospital have simply been transferred to the county jail.

Finally, the public housing complex is the new great hope, and fastest-growing public expenditure, for the homeless. Like most West Coast cities, San Francisco has gone all in on "Housing First," the theory that the municipal government must provide free housing for the homeless in perpetuity, with no expectations of sobriety, work, or participation in rehabilitation programs. For a city with a recurring homeless population of 18,000, this is an enormous expense.[8] In 2019, San Francisco spent $285 million on shelters and "permanent supportive housing," plus $65 million on traditional public housing, vouchers, and single-room-occupancy units.[9] At the same time, voters passed an additional $600 million bond to build "affordable housing." But still, 67 percent of the Bay Area's homeless are unsheltered.[10]

On the surface, all of the various reports, task forces, and audits pay their respects to "evidence-based interventions," "data-driven solutions," and "best practices." However, even on its own terms, as partisans on all sides have slowly conceded, the technical approach to homelessness has failed. The experts have built a massive, multibillion-dollar apparatus that spans across medical, carceral, and social services, but the system is overloaded and even its partisans must now admit that it has failed to reduce homelessness.

The question that dominates the current public discourse is what is to be done. To their credit, San Francisco's leaders have recognized the failure of the current system and proposed an ambitious reform agenda. However, in broad terms, this agenda only deepens its dependency on the social-scientific model and doubles-down on its worst assumptions. It can be summarized this way: deinstitutionalization, destigmatization, and decriminalization.

In 2019, Mayor Breed and Supervisors Matt Haney and Hilary Ronen passed legislation for sweeping "mental health reform." The plan would increase total spending on mental health and substance abuse to $500 million per year, and prioritize the homeless, create a central service center, and pressure private insurers to cover more costs. When it passed unanimously through the Board of Supervisors, Ronen celebrated it as a progressive milestone: "We just created the first universal mental health and substance use system in the country."[11]

But this universality is only a theoretical formulation. The legislation does not include a funding source and, more importantly, simply expands the existing behavioral health system, rather than reforming it. For the perilous trifecta, the problem is often not access to services but participation in services. According to the latest one-night count, only 17 percent of the homeless reported using mental health services and 11 percent reported using substance abuse services. For the unsheltered population, these figures are almost certainly lower.[12]

The problem is that members of the perilous trifecta are the least likely to seek services. According to the Treatment Advocacy Center, approximately 40 percent to 50 percent of patients with schizophrenia and bipolar disorder suffer from anosognosia, which is the inability to understand their own disorder. This often leads to a refusal to enter treatment and take medication. Adding a serious addiction to methamphetamine, which can cause paranoia, psychosis, hallucinations, and violent behavior, only compounds the problem.[13]

In the past, the solution to this paradox was compulsion. The state took custody of the "gravely disabled" and treated them in long-term residential institutions. However, with the exposure of civil rights abuses and the release of *One Flew Over the Cuckoo's Nest*, the United States gradually dismantled its mental health system, reducing the number of mental health beds per capita by an astonishing 95 percent between 1955 and 2016.[14] Today, California has fewer beds per capita than the national average, with San Francisco having only 237 adult psychiatric beds available at a given time – drastically insufficient for the number of people in need.[15]

Although Mayor Breed has tentatively moved toward a return to short-term "conservatorships," a form of involuntary commitment for individuals who present a grave danger to themselves or others, the plan has neither the scope nor the force to significantly reduce the numbers of the perilous trifecta. Because of pressure from disability activists and the ACLU, which has called conservatorships "the greatest deprivation of civil liberties aside from the death penalty," the plan is limited to individuals who have had eight or more involuntary psychiatric holds in the past year, which, in practice, would mean fewer than 100 people citywide.[16]

At bottom, San Francisco's mental health policy is constrained by its own ideological priorities. Despite good intentions, political leaders in San Francisco have confused compassion with public expenditure, hoping that creating more shelters and treatment programs will induce the perilous trifecta into the social-scientific apparatus. At the same time, under the spell of the civil libertarians, they have refused to abandon the fundamental premises of deinstitutionalization, believing that the homeless have a "human right" to languish in the streets.

No matter how much it spends on treatment programs, the city must ultimately resolve the paradox of the perilous trifecta. Will the addicts brazenly shooting up in the subway station seek treatment on their own?[17] Will the woman eating rats in the alleyway voluntarily accept help?[18] We already know the answer to these questions, but the political class's conception of freedom, drenched in the Molotov rags of Berkeley 1968, cannot admit that a successful policy will require force. Until it does, however, the perilous trifecta will continue to dominate life on the streets.

If anything, the progressive-socialists argue, there is already too much force in the system. The newly elected district attorney, Chesa Boudin, has promised to lead a "decarceral movement," substantially reducing the county jail population, ending cash bail, and decriminalizing quality-of-life crimes associated with homelessness, including public camping, drug consumption, prostitution, and public urination.[19] Boudin contends that the criminal justice system in San Francisco is a domain of persistent inequalities – locking up a disproportionate number of poor and minority residents – and has become the dumping ground for the addicted and mentally ill.[20] Rather than continue this system, Boudin argues, the city must "implement a comprehensive transformation of the criminal justice system to decriminalize and treat mental illness, housing instability, and substance use as public health issues rather than criminal justice issues."[21]

There is an element of truth to Boudin's formulation. According to a single-day snapshot of the San Francisco County Jail population, 48 percent of inmates were African American, 70 percent self-reported substance abuse, and 10 percent were deemed to have a serious mental illness.[22] However, the narrative that the city is deliberately targeting nonviolent drug offenders and "criminalizing homeless" is patently false. The snapshot shows that 68 percent of inmates were arrested for violence, weapons, and serious felonies; contrary to progressive rhetoric, only 4 percent were arrested for drug crimes – a vanishingly small number of people for a city in the midst of a heroin and methamphetamine epidemic.

The experts have built a massive, multibillion-dollar apparatus that spans across medical, carceral, and social services, but the system is overloaded and even its partisans must now admit that it has failed to reduce homelessness.

The hard reality is that the perilous trifecta has fueled a boom in property crime, public disorder, and violence. In 2019, at least 1,120 individuals in the perilous trifecta spent time in the county jail.[23] The city currently has the highest property crime rate in the nation and, even with the existing level of enforcement, which progressives denounce as "overpolicing," has enabled massive open-air drug markets in neighborhoods such as the Tenderloin, which is a central hub for the homeless population.[24] Although it has become a taboo among the progressive intelligentsia, the nexus between homelessness, addiction, and crime is clear. According to city and federal data, virtually all of the unsheltered homeless are unemployed, while at the same time, those with serious addictions spend an average of $1,256 to $1,834 a month on methamphetamine and heroin.[25] With no legitimate source of income, many addicts support their habit through a "hustle," which can include theft, fraud, prostitution, and other property crimes.

Boudin's plan for "mass decarceration," which appeals to the fallacy that crime can be solved through social services alone, amounts to a reverse Broken Windows theory and would almost certainly lead to an increase in the overall crime rate. This principle can be illustrated with an especially pernicious crime in San Francisco: car break-ins. In 2019, the city had an incredible 25,667 "smash-and-grabs," as thieves sought valuables and other property to sell on the black market.[26] Rather than attempt to prevent or even disincentivize this crime, Boudin has proposed a $1.5 million fund to pay for auto glass repair, arguing that it "will help put money into San Francisco jobs and San Francisco businesses."[27] In literal terms, Boudin is subsidizing broken windows, under the absurd notion that it can be transformed into a Keynesian job-creation program.

If Boudin can implement his policy vision, what would it mean for the perilous trifecta? Its numbers would increase, perhaps dramatically. According to a scathing front-page editorial in the *San Francisco Chronicle*, the city already attracts 450 chronically homeless individuals from outside its boundaries each year, in part because of San Francisco's reputation as "a sanctuary" for people who want to live on the streets and "flout the law with impunity."[28] Under Boudin's utopian vision of mass decriminalization, the signal would be even stronger: San Francisco has the ideal policy conditions to sleep on the streets, feed an addiction, and commit property crimes to survive – with little or no enforcement from the state.

The implicit wager of San Francisco's policy is that the social-scientific apparatus can rescue people faster than the perilous trifecta expands its ranks. But the evidence points toward a gloomier outcome. Methamphetamine deaths increased 500 percent from 2008 to 2018.[29] Fentanyl overdoses doubled in 2019 over the year before.[30] Meanwhile, the socialized state has reached a point of near exhaustion. First responders, police officers, and emergency room nurses are burning out. Psychiatrists at San Francisco General Hospital despair about the mass migration of out-of-state residents in search of the "San Francisco Special": "housing, a psychiatrist, case manager, primary care provider, and transfer of Medicaid or general assistance."[31]

The final plank of San Francisco's policy platform is destigmatization. Public health experts in the city have gradually abandoned recovery and sobriety as the ideal outcome, preferring the limited goal of "harm reduction."[32] In a recent task force report on methamphetamine, the San Francisco Department of Public Health noted that meth users "are likely to experience high levels of stigma and rejection in their personal and social lives," which are "often reinforced by language and media portrayals depicting individuals who use alongside images of immorality, having chaotic lives, and perpetual use."[33]

On the surface, this is a strange contention. If San Francisco's perilous trifecta is any guide, methamphetamine use heavily correlates with chaotic lives, perpetual use, and various transgressions against traditional morality. The harm reductionists' argument, however, rests on the belief that addiction is an involuntary brain disease, akin to Alzheimer's or dementia. In their view, addiction is better seen as a disability, and any stigma associated with it is therefore an act of ignorance and cruelty. According to the Department of Public Health, the goal of harm reduction policy is to reduce this unjustified stigma and focus public policy on "non-abstinence-based residential treatment programs," "supervised injection services," "trauma-informed sobering site[s]," and "training for staff on how to engage marginalized or vulnerable communities in ways that do not perpetuate trauma or stigma."[34]

In practice, the task force recommendations would create an entire infrastructure to service addiction, rather than to reduce it. Although proponents of harm reduction claim the mantle of compassion, it's a deeply fatalistic theory. It assumes that most people cannot recover from serious addiction and, therefore, the social obligation is to provide the space and resources for addicts to pursue their own ends, which, for 40 percent of the perilous trifecta population, means 13 or more years in and out of homelessness.[35] Activists have suggested that addicts can "reduce harms" by "[using] indoors instead of on the street," "reducing how much [they are] using," "transitioning from injecting to smoking," and "continuing to use one type of drug but quitting another drug."[36] But in the face of the pathological overload of the perilous trifecta, these recommendations are negligently naïve, relegating a large portion of the homeless to a lifetime of chaos, sickness, and despair.

In the long term, the real danger of destigmatization is that it would lead to the complete normalization of serious addiction and its consequences. Although intellectuals have sought to destroy stigma and "shame culture" for more than a half century, these social forces have served a purpose throughout time: to prevent the stigmatized behavior and protect the community from the danger of contagion. In San Francisco, progressives have attempted to normalize the worst aspects of street homelessness, minimizing the drug use, toxic waste, psychotic episodes, and related crimes; they have blurred the lines between sickness and health, madness and sanity. Moreover, without a trace of irony, they have weaponized destigmatization itself, shaming anyone who opposes the breakdown of public order as "fascists" and "homeless haters."

In broad terms, the political class has insisted on greater control over the corporations, developers, and landlords while deregulating life at the bottom. The result has been a deepening inequality and an even more anarchic world for the poor. There is an entire social media community of mostly anonymous accounts which documents the squalor of the encampments and psychotic episodes in the streets; it is the last resistance to the normalization of the perilous trifecta. Participants maintain their anonymity, it seems, out of fear of retribution. It's a dark reality, but perhaps it's a warning of what's to come.[37]

In the end, San Francisco finds itself fighting a monster. "Homelessness isn't just a problem; it's a symptom," says Mayor Breed. "The symptom of unaffordable housing, of income inequality, of institutional racism, of addiction, untreated illness, and decades of disinvestment. These are the problems. And if we're going to fight homelessness, we've got to fight them all."[38] But this is part of the reason homelessness has become so intractable – the political class has haunted its own world with abstractions; it has projected its own ideological premises onto the brutal reality of the streets.

The city must let go of its sacred beliefs – that homelessness is predominantly about capitalism, housing, and racism, and that it can be rectified through applied social science – and address the clear evidence that homelessness is the endpoint of a deeper anomie, the generalized breakdown of the social order that can be reversed only through profound cultural reform. Until this reckoning comes, San Francisco will continue to become a city for the affluent and the indigent, divided between those who can navigate the postmodern world and those who are broken under its weight. It will be caught in the eternal recurrence of overdoses, deaths, violence, and the public degradation of human life.

The only way forward for the men and women of the perilous trifecta is to recognize that society must reestablish a sense of restraint. The appeal of San Francisco is that it has long been a city that demolishes limits, from the cultural breakthroughs of the beats and hippies to the technological breakthroughs of the computer age. But political leaders must recognize that there is a social cost when the destruction of limits goes too far; they must accept that disorder is not freedom, that chaos is not liberty.

Fifty years ago, Joan Didion chronicled the early emergence of this crisis. In her essay "Slouching Towards Bethlehem," Didion brings us face-to-face with a five-year-old girl named Susan, whose parents had been giving her acid and peyote for the past year. The little girl "likes Coca-Cola, ice cream, Marty in the Jefferson Airplane, [and] Bob in the Grateful Dead," and tells us that her classmates Sally and Anne also get stoned.[39]

Boudin's plan for "mass decarceration," which appeals to the fallacy that crime can be solved through social services alone, amounts to a reverse broken windows theory and would almost certainly lead to an increase in the overall crime rate.

Whenever I find myself on the streets of San Francisco in the present day, I wonder how many of the men and women folded over on the sidewalks are the children of Susan, Sally, and Anne, born into this cruel tableau of shattered norms and shattered minds. I try to listen to them when they pace across the street screaming, hoping to glean some insight from their verbal tics and meth-induced psychoses. It seems that they, too, are fighting a monster, but one that is much deeper and more complex than the political class can admit.

Sadly, as in the heyday of the Haight-Ashbury, San Francisco continues to attract the homeless, the addicted, and the insane. There is already a steady migration of chronically homeless individuals into the city each year. Until the political leadership changes its current policies, it will find what it is seeking – a world without limits, in which pathologies are rationalized and public nightmares are explained away. The city can build new housing units, fortify its public spaces, and streamline its bureaucracy, but the social science imperative cannot fix, or even comprehend, what has gone wrong in San Francisco.

PRICED OUT OF SHELTER AND ONTO THE STREETS

How California's Housing Crisis Has Pushed Thousands into Homelessness and Has Many More on the Brink

WAYNE WINEGARDEN

AN EVALUATION OF California's homelessness crisis is incomplete without also considering the state's unaffordable cost of living and crushing level of poverty.[1] The state's unaffordability problem is widespread. It begins with the excessive amount of money families must pay to either rent a residence or finance a mortgage. It also includes the excessive cost to purchase basic necessities, particularly energy and food. Due to these costs, an income that could comfortably support a family in most metropolitan areas outside the state is barely enough to cover the basic living expenses in California. The exorbitant amount of money needed to purchase necessities also feeds the pervasive poverty problem that continues to worsen in California despite the state's long-term growth in wealth.

These problems contribute to the state's homelessness both directly and indirectly. Directly, these costs price people out of their homes. Indirectly, because of the high cost of living, too many Californians are living paycheck to paycheck. While getting by, their housing security is tenuous. One adverse life event – perhaps a medical emergency, an expensive car repair, or a divorce – can start a vicious cycle that ultimately leads to homelessness.

Since the lack of affordability has pushed people to the financial edge, it is a tragic reality that too many Californians have been driven into homelessness due to unexpected financial costs that families in other states would be able to withstand. As the risk of homelessness will persist so long as so many families are living on the edge, California's unique homelessness problem will not be sustainably addressed until the policies that are pricing people out of their homes are changed.

California's Homelessness Was Rising
While the Economy Was Growing

Figure 6.1 demonstrates that California's homelessness crisis was not always different from the rest of the country. According to HUD, between 2007 and 2014 the number of homeless people in the US was declining 1.3 percent per year. Consistent with the progress nationally, the number of homeless in California was also declining by an even larger 2.8 percent annually. By 2014, there were more than 25,000 fewer homeless people in California than in 2007.

Figure 6.1. Total Point-in-Time (PIT) Homeless Count: California Compared to Rest of the Country, 2007–2019

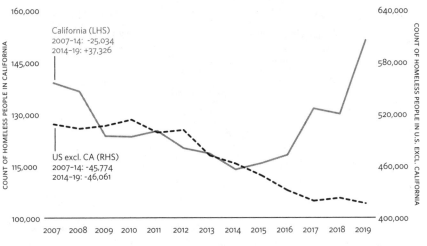

Source: HUD

But something changed in 2014.

Outside of California, the number of homeless people continued to decline, and even more quickly. The decline in the number of homeless people in the US outside of California increased by 2.1 percent per year between 2014 and 2019. Unlike the rest of the country, and during a period of economic growth, progress in reducing the number of homeless people in California suddenly ended after 2014.

As of 2019, there were more than 37,000 additional homeless people in California compared to 2014 – a dismal 5.8 percent annual increase – also eclipsing the number of homeless following the Great

Recession. While not visualized in figure 6.1, the HUD data illustrate that California is one of the few states that has seen the homeless population reach new highs as of 2019.

Figure 6.2 demonstrates that this growth in California's homeless problem that began after 2014 has mostly occurred in three regions: the Los Angeles metro area, the Bay Area, and Silicon Valley. The surges in these three zones accounted for 79 percent of the state's increase in the homeless population.

Figure 6.2. Change in PIT Homeless Population Between 2014 and 2019, Select California Regions

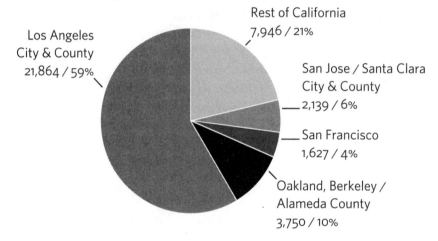

Rest of California
7,946 / 21%

Los Angeles
City & County
21,864 / 59%

San Jose / Santa Clara
City & County
2,139 / 6%

San Francisco
1,627 / 4%

Oakland, Berkeley /
Alameda County
3,750 / 10%

Source: Author calculations based on HUD data

It is important to note that these three regions' share of the growth in the homeless population is disproportionate to their share of the homeless population. As of 2014, these regions accounted for 46 percent of California's homeless population, which obviously grew, reaching 54 percent of the state's homeless population in 2019. The fact that the Los Angeles area, the Bay Area, and Silicon Valley represent nearly 80 percent of the growth in homelessness since 2014, but a bit more than 50 percent of the state's total homeless population, demonstrates that something has changed for the worse in these regions. While some differences have nothing to do with economics, one common factor across all of these regions has been a material increase in the already out-of-control cost of living that is literally pricing people out of their homes.

High Cost of Living

When all costs are considered, living expenses in California are significantly higher than the rest of the country. Research by the Federal Reserve Bank of St. Louis (FRB-SL) documents just how expensive the Golden State is.[2]

The FRB-SL estimates regional price parities (RPPs) for each state and large metropolitan statistical areas (MSAs) based on data from the Bureau of Economic Analysis (BEA). The RPPs are a measure for comparing the cost of living across the 50 states. As constructed, the average cost of living in the US is scaled to 100. A value above 100 indicates the cost of living is higher than average in that state or MSA, whereas a value below 100 indicates the cost of living is less. Based on the data for 2018, California (114.8) is the fourth most expensive place to live in the US behind Hawaii (118.5), Washington, D.C. (116.9), and New York (115.8). While all costs are above average, the largest drivers of California's excessive costs are rent and housing expenses.

The consequence of this elevated cost of living is that California's median income is not as high as it appears. According to the US Census, the median household income in California was $70,038 in 2017 and $70,489 in 2018.[3] This was high enough to be the twelfth and thirteenth highest average household income in the country for each year, respectively. But the median household income data do not account for the differences in the cost of living between the states.

Since the lack of affordability has pushed people to the financial edge, it is a tragic reality that too many Californians have been driven into homelessness due to unexpected financial costs that families in other states would be able to withstand.

To account for the divergence in the cost of living, the FRB-SL study adjusted the median household income for each state in 2017 for the buying power of that income. Adjusted for buying power, California's median household income was estimated to be $58,967 in 2017 – 15.8 percent lower than the official estimate from the US Census. This adjustment also drops California's ranking. Adjusting the state's twelfth highest income for how far that income goes, the purchasing power of California's median income is only the twenty-fourth highest in the country. Once adjusted for California's high cost of living, the state falls from an above-average income state to simply average.

Yet measuring the excessive costs statewide underestimates the cost-of-living problems. As figure 6.2 demonstrates, nearly 80 percent of the growth in the homeless population is concentrated in the Los Angeles metro area, the San Jose metro area, and the Bay Area. The cost-of-living problems in these areas are worse than the statewide average. To get a sense of how large these problems are, table 6.1 compares the cost-adjusted incomes as measured by the FRB-SL cost-of-living calculator in these three California regions to two other geographical areas: Springfield, Missouri, and Austin, Texas. Springfield is chosen to represent the cost of living in a typical area. Austin is chosen because it is a growing tech cluster and, consequently, a competitor city to San Francisco and Silicon Valley. Comparing the actual median household income in the regions at the center of California's homeless crisis to the equivalent cost-adjusted income in these comparator cities demonstrates just how bad California's unaffordability problem is.

Table 6.1. Cost of Living Equivalent Incomes:
San Francisco–Oakland–Hayward, San Jose, and Los Angeles
Compared to Springfield, MO, and Austin, TX

MEDIAN HOUSEHOLD INCOME BASIS,
5-year median income, 2014–2018

	San Francisco–Oakland–Hayward $104,552	San Jose metro $104,234	Los Angeles metro $64,251
Adjusted Income			
Springfield, MO	$71,063	$69,277	$47,736
Austin, TX	$82,090	$80,027	$55,143
Percentage Reduction			
Springfield, MO	-32.0%	-33.5%	-25.7%
Austin, TX	-21.5%	-23.2%	-14.2%

Source: Federal Reserve Bank of St. Louis, Cost of Living Calculator

Taking the San Jose conversion as the example, the 5-year average median household income in that area between 2014 and 2018 was $104,234. However, in Austin, a household can have the exact same standard of living if their income was $80,027 – 23 percent lower. A household in Springfield could have the same standard of living with an even lower income of $69,277. Overall, compared to these three regions in California, a household's income could be between 14 percent and 34 percent lower in these comparative cities while still maintaining the same standard of living.

Even California's high salaries for tech workers are much lower than they appear due to the state's high cost of living. For example, the Bay Area pays its tech workers an average annual salary of $155,000 – $9,000 higher than the US market average.[4] However, once the Bay Area's high cost of living is incorporated, workers in the region are actually earning less than their peers. Illustrating this problem, in its annual "State of Salaries" report, Hired (a job-matching company), asked, "How much further do average tech salaries stretch in other cities compared to San Francisco?"[5] The average tech worker in Austin, for example, would need to earn an additional $87,000 to maintain their current standard of living in San Francisco.[6] Table 6.2 illustrates that, once adjusted for San Francisco's cost of living, tech salaries in the Bay Area go from the highest to next to the lowest.

Due to the imbalance between San Francisco's pay premium and its high cost of living, there is still a "large differential between what's needed for a comfortable life versus what people earn."[7] A single person needs to earn at least $110,000 a year "to live comfortably" in the Bay Area.[8] More than half of that sum ($61,634) is needed to pay for necessities such as housing, groceries, health care, utilities, and transportation.[9] As an example of these excessive costs, residents "pay the highest premium for groceries" in the country, "almost $500 a month."[10]

As another example, the Council for Community and Economic Research Cost of Living Index ranks the "regional differences in the cost of consumer goods and services, excluding taxes and non-consumer expenditures."[11] The index includes measures for more than "90,000 prices covering almost 60 different items," such as "housing, utilities, grocery items, transportation, health care, and miscellaneous goods and services."

Table 6.2. Annual Average Tech Salaries Adjusted for Cost of Living

	Average Annual Salary	Salary Adjusted for Bay Area Cost of Living	Necessary Raise
Austin	$137,000	$224,000	$87,000
Denver	$126,000	$202,000	$76,000
Seattle	$142,000	$188,000	$46,000
Chicago	$124,000	$187,000	$63,000
Los Angeles	$137,000	$182,000	$45,000
Boston	$136,000	$173,000	$37,000
Washington, D.C.	$131,000	$158,000	$27,000
SF Bay Area	$155,000	$155,000	$0
New York	$143,000	$141,000	-$2,000

Source: Federal Reserve Bank of St. Louis, Cost of Living Calculator

As of the first quarter of 2020, three California regions qualified for the top 10 most expensive urban areas, according to the index. San Francisco is the third most expensive urban area to live in, behind only the Manhattan borough of New York City and Honolulu. Oakland, California, is the seventh most expensive area and Orange County is the ninth most expensive. These figures are not adjusted for California's high tax burden, which only increases costs for people in California.

Many other cost-of-living indices confirm these results. In its grading of the states, CNBC ranked California as the second most expensive state in the country, with only Hawaii having a higher cost of living.[12] In an analysis of 2018 data, *U.S. News & World Report* ranked California as the second least-affordable state in the country (Hawaii was once again the most expensive) based on a combined assessment of the state's housing affordability and cost of living.[13] World Population Review, an independent provider of global demographic data, ranked the cost of living across the 50 states and Washington, D.C., based on the costs of groceries, housing, utilities, and transportation.[14] Accounting for all of these costs, California ranked as the third most expensive state behind Washington, D.C. (included with the states) and Hawaii.

These data and surveys confirm that California's cost of living is exceptionally high. But from a homelessness perspective, understanding the impact from these excessive cost burdens on lower-income families is particularly important. One way to account for the cost-of-living impact on lower-income families is to compare California's supplemental poverty rate (SPM) to the official poverty rate.[15] The SPM adjusts the official poverty rate to incorporate the value of non-cash income support benefits, the costs of medical care, and work-related expenses. Of particular relevance for California, the SPM also adjusts for the cost-of-living differences across geographies.

The SPM provides an important perspective on the number of people struggling with poverty, particularly for high-cost California, because the official poverty rate is based on a fixed income and expense threshold that is applied across the entire country. The SPM accounts for the reality that salaries do not go far in many parts of California compared to the rest of the country. And accounting for this reality demonstrates that there are significantly more people living on the edge in California that the official poverty measure fails to recognize.

Accounting for California's exceptionally high cost of living, a total of 7.1 million people living in the state (18.1 percent) are in poverty. Compared to the official poverty measure (which finds 4.9 million people or 12.5 percent of Californians live in poverty), the SPM measure demonstrates that the state's poverty problem is much more pervasive than acknowledged. This gap means that the income of 2.2 million Californians is insufficient to escape poverty but would be sufficient if they lived in most other states.

Importantly, the amount of poverty induced by the state's high cost of living is larger than any other state or the District of Columbia, whether measured by the 2.2 million increase in the number of people living in poverty or the 5.6 percentage point increase in the poverty rate. More astonishingly, the 2.2 million increase in the number

The SPM accounts for the reality that salaries do not go far in many parts of California compared to the rest of the country. And accounting for this reality demonstrates that there are significantly more people living on the edge in California that the official poverty measure fails to recognize.

of poor people in California accounts for 81 percent of the 2.7 million additional people nationwide living in poverty, according to the SPM.

Recognizing that California's high cost of living forces more people below the poverty line fundamentally changes our understanding of poverty in the state. Not only does California have the highest poverty rate of any state in the nation (Washington, D.C., has a higher poverty rate, 18.2 percent), but it accounts for 17 percent of the people living in poverty nationwide and 25 to 30 percent of the nation's homeless population, even though the state accounts for only 12 percent of the nation's population.[16] Such a disproportionate amount of people living on the financial edge means that there is a higher proportion of people who are at high risk of becoming homeless should an adverse life event happen to them.

Declining Affordability, Rising Homelessness

Whether it is the Bay Area, Silicon Valley, or the Los Angeles metro area, the high cost of living in the regions where most of the spike in the homelessness population has occurred is infamous. Importantly, leading up to the 2014 spike in homelessness, the unaffordability of housing and the costs for electricity, gasoline, and other necessities also took a sustained turn for the worse. This simultaneity is no mere coincidence.

Starting with housing costs, a general rule of thumb states that households should obey the 30 percent rule – essentially, households should not spend more than 30 percent of their gross income on rent or mortgage costs. While some financial planners have argued that more flexibility is required when applying the 30 percent rule,[17] for lower-income households this flexibility typically means that they should be spending less than 30 percent of their income for housing costs, not more. Moreover, nationally, the required spending that a median household needs to devote to pay a mortgage for a median house tends to return to that 30 percent threshold. Compared to the housing affordability in the US, California's housing unaffordability is in the stratosphere – particularly in the Bay Area and Silicon Valley.

To get a sense of how unaffordable housing costs are in California, consider that the median household income in San Francisco in 2018 was $110,601, which is 75 percent higher than the median household income in the US in 2018 ($63,179).[18] From a housing affordability perspective, the problem is that the median price for a home in San Francisco was $1.6 million in 2018, which was 384 percent higher than the median price for a home in the US ($325,275).[19] As a result, based on the 30-year fixed mortgage rate in 2018,[20] a mortgage payment for the median-priced home in San Francisco was a ridiculous 87 percent of the median family's income, compared to the mortgage payment for the median-priced home in the US, which was 32 percent (or around the 30 percent rule). Such an outrageous unaffordability level in San Francisco is clearly unsustainable.

Figure 6.3 replicates this affordability calculation for the Los Angeles, San Francisco, Alameda, and Santa Clara metro areas between 1990 and 2019. The resulting housing affordability levels in these regions are compared to the housing affordability in California and the average US housing affordability. Housing affordability in the US has sometimes surged above the 30 percent affordability rule since 1990, but over time the average housing costs in the US returns to the 30 percent level.

This has not been the case in California, nor in the three regions that are driving the homeless crisis in the state. Starting with the overall state trends, the costs of owning a median-priced home started approaching the 30 percent affordability level following the

Figure 6.3. Housing Affordability: US, California, and Select Cities, 1990-2019

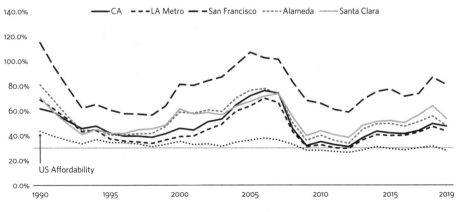

Source: Author calculations based on HUD data

housing bust in the early 2010s. The median house even became affordable, briefly, in 2011 and 2012. Unlike the median affordability level in the US – where housing has remained around the 30 percent level – housing affordability started degrading in 2012, reaching an estimated 48 percent in 2019; paying the costs for a 30-year fixed mortgage for the median-priced Californian home requires 48 percent of the median households' income.

From a housing affordability perspective, the problem is that the median price for a home in San Francisco was $1.6 million in 2018, which was 384 percent higher than the median price for a home in the US ($325,275).

The affordability trends in the Los Angeles metro area have closely mirrored the California average, and as of 2019 the affordability level reached an expensive 44 percent. However challenging the unaffordability problem in the Los Angeles metro area is, it is significantly worse in the Bay Area and Silicon Valley. As figure 6.3 illustrates, while affordability improved following the housing bust, homes in these regions still remained painfully unaffordable. Worse, just as with the broader California trends, housing unaffordability in the Bay Area and Silicon Valley also started worsening beginning around 2012. Based on the estimated values in 2019, the affordability levels are once again approaching the unaffordable levels associated with the housing bubble of the early twenty-first century in both the Bay Area and Silicon Valley.

California's worsening housing affordability since 2012 is just one of the major costs of living that has significantly risen along with the spike in homelessness. Another is electricity costs. While Californians living along the coast benefit from the state's more temperate climate that reduces their use of electricity, not all residents do. Those residents who do not benefit face a higher financial burden from the state's traditionally high electricity costs per kilowatt-hour (kWh).

Beginning in 2012, California's traditionally expensive electricity costs began to become even more burdensome compared to the average electricity costs in the US (see figure 6.4). According to the Energy Information Administration (EIA), Californians paid 13.5¢ per kWh for electricity in 2012, which was 37.2 percent more expensive than the US average.[21] Between 2012 and 2018 (the latest data available), electricity costs per kWh rose 7 percent in the US, to 10.53¢ per kWh in 2018. Electricity costs in California, in contrast, increased

22.8 percent between 2012 and 2018 and now are 16.58¢ per kWh for electricity, one of the most expensive rates in the country. As figure 6.4 notes, due to these diverging price growth trends, electricity costs are now 57.5 percent more expensive in California than in the rest of the country.

Figure 6.4. California's Excessive Retail Electricity Prices Compared to the US Average, 1990-2019

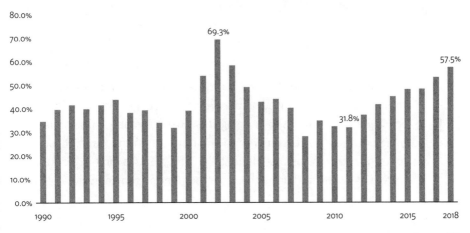

Source: EIA

As a result of these high retail electricity prices, and despite California's temperate climate – meaning there is less need for people to run air conditioners and heaters as intensely as people living in the Deep South or Northeast – California's estimated monthly electricity costs of $164.51 were among the top 10 in the country.[22]

In addition to electricity, gasoline prices are also among the most expensive in the nation – second only to Hawaii.[23] Since most of California's premium is due to its policies, the variation between cities within the state pales in comparison to the gap between California and the rest of the country. More pertinent for the state's homeless crisis, the cost of gasoline spiked in 2015 relative to the cost in the rest of the country (see figure 6.5).[24]

California's higher rent, electricity, and gas prices are essential inputs into most other goods and services. As a consequence, these higher costs drive up prices across the state's economy. With respect to the homelessness crisis, the adverse impact on grocery prices is

Figure 6.5. California's Excessive Gasoline Prices Compared to the US Average, 2001–2019

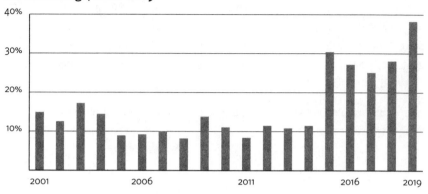

Source: EIA

particularly troubling. According to lovemoney.com, which ranked each of the 50 states based on the average cost of grocery prices (50 being the most expensive, 1 being the most affordable), California, while not the most expensive, was number 40 on the list.[25] These costs further reduce the affordability of California and create a regressive cost that harms the larger number of people living at or near the poverty line.

Declining Affordability Is Behind California's Rising Homelessness

There are many adverse consequences from California's high cost of living, and the rising problem of homelessness is one of them. Consider the results from a 2017 survey in San Francisco that assess the primary causes of homelessness.[26] According to the survey, more than a third – 34 percent – of the homeless are on the streets in San Francisco due to direct economic reasons. Twenty-two percent became homeless because of job loss, while 12 percent were evicted.

These survey results are not unique. LA Family Housing, an organization dedicated to helping people "transition out of homelessness and poverty," states that while "the causes can vary widely," it is still evident that "often homelessness and poverty are inextricably linked. People who are poor are frequently unable to pay for necessities such as housing, food, childcare, health care, and education. Being poor can mean a person is one illness, one accident, or one paycheck away from living on the streets."[27]

Table 6.3. Primary Causes of Homelessness in San Francisco, 2017

Reason	Share
Lost job	22%
Alcohol/drugs	15%
Argument/family or friend who asked them to leave	13%
Eviction	12%
Divorce/separation	10%
Illness or medical problem	7%

Source: Applied Survey Research

The US Conference of Mayors' annual survey has "consistently found the lack of affordable housing to be the *leading cause of homelessness.*"[28] The National Law Center on Homelessness and Poverty concurs with this conclusion, claiming that "insufficient income and lack of affordable housing are the leading causes of homelessness."[29] CalMatters similarly cites California's increasing unaffordability as a primary driver of the state's worst-in-the-country homelessness crisis:

> Mental health problems, addiction, childhood trauma, interaction with the criminal justice system and poverty all play significant roles in whether someone becomes homeless. But the primary reason? They can no longer afford rent. About 1.3 million California renter households are considered "extremely low income," making less than $25,000 a year, according to the California Housing Partnership, a nonprofit organization the state created to advise affordable housing builders. Predictably, these financially strapped households can barely afford the state's escalating rents, and are most at risk of falling into homelessness.[30]

Putting these analyses together with the affordability data reviewed above confirms this story. Whichever measure is used, the cost of living in California is one of the most expensive in the nation. Furthermore, California's unaffordability worsened at the same time that the number of people who fell into homelessness began its sustained rise. The simultaneity of these trends is not coincidental. California has the largest homelessness crisis because it is one of the least-affordable states in the nation. The two problems are intrinsically intertwined.

Due to this interdependency, sustainably solving the state's worst-in-the-nation homelessness crisis requires policy reforms that address the root causes of the affordability crisis.

As will be discussed in chapter 10, there is no inherent reason why California should be unaffordable. Instead, California's cost of living is so unaffordable because a myriad of policies imposes tremendous costs on all residents of the state. While these costs may be manageable by higher-income families, they push lower-income families to the financial brink. The rising number of homeless includes, in part, those who have been unlucky enough to be pushed too far.

JUDICIAL INTERVENTIONISM

How Court Rulings Change How Cities Enforce
"Quality of Life" Laws

7

JOSEPH TARTAKOVSKY

THE MODERN ERA OF "quality of life" laws arose after the abolition of vagrancy and loitering laws by the early 1970s. These quality of life laws, usually narrow and specific, today govern the conduct most commonly associated with individuals experiencing homelessness. The modern jurisprudence on quality of life laws is the product of decades of test cases, largely beginning in the 1990s, challenging every variety of law bearing on the conduct of those living on the streets or in their cars.[1] Most of these lawsuits were brought by homeless-rights activists, often aided by the nation's largest law firms or law school clinics.[2] They have attacked such laws under the First Amendment (guaranteeing free expression), Fourth Amendment (protecting against unlawful searches and seizures), Eighth Amendment (forbidding "cruel and unusual" punishment), and Fourteenth Amendment (securing property and certain procedural rights). The discussion below examines how courts have defined the limits imposed by the US Constitution on mostly municipal quality of life laws.

Camping or Sleeping in Public

The National Law Center on Homelessness and Poverty, a leading homeless-rights advocacy organization, surveyed 187 cities and found that some 34 percent have specific citywide bans on camping; another 57 percent have bans on camping in a particular public place.[3] The Center claims that citywide camping bans are up 60 percent since 2011. That may be so, but these particular laws did not emerge from some newfound public anxiety about street camping. Rather these new "anti-camping" laws address the concerns formerly enforced by anti-vagrancy laws. The form of the law is new; the policy is old.

61

Part II: How California Became First in Homelessness

In 1968, Los Angeles declared, rather ambitiously, that a person shall not "sleep in or upon any street, sidewalk or other public way."[4] Decades later, the law was successfully challenged by homeless persons who received citations under the law. In *Jones v. City of Los Angeles* (2006), the US Court of Appeals for the Ninth Circuit, the federal appeals court covering the western United States, forbid the city from enforcing the law as written.[5] The court called the law "one of the most restrictive municipal laws regulating public spaces in the United States" – insofar as it outlawed sitting, lying, or sleeping at any time, citywide – even though sleep, the court continued, is a "universal and unavoidable consequence of being human."[6] The court's view was that the law left homeless individuals in an impossible position – sleep or get ticketed – and that this violated the cruel and unusual punishments clause of the Eighth Amendment. Yet the decision was vacated a year and a half later, when Los Angeles settled the dispute by agreeing not to enforce the law between 9 P.M. and 6 A.M., except within 10 feet of entrances, driveways, and loading docks, and not until 1,250 units of supportive housing were built, half of those units near Skid Row.[7]

So matters stood until the momentous decision in *Martin v. City of Boise* in 2018.[8] There the Ninth Circuit not only revived the vacated *Jones* decision but went even further. The suit arose in Boise, Idaho, when six homeless individuals challenged a Boise ordinance that barred the use of "streets, sidewalks, parks or public places as a camping place at any time."[9] "Camping," in turn, was defined as the "use of public property" as a "dwelling" or as a "living accommodation" at any time between "sunset and sunrise."[10] The court adopted the reasoning of the *Jones* decision: that "human beings are biologically compelled to rest" and so a city "may not criminalize conduct that is an unavoidable consequence of being homeless – namely sitting, lying, or sleeping on the streets."[11] This, again, was held to violate the cruel and unusual punishments clause.

As it happens, within months after the Boise complaint was first filed in 2009, the City of Boise revised its policy: it would *decline* to enforce the ordinance on evenings where no shelter beds were available (as determined by a daily tally communicated to police). But the court found this insufficient, since counting beds alone did not account for whether that bed was actually accessible to a particular homeless individual. (More on this below.) So the court devised its "practically available" standard – its innovation over *Jones*. *Jones* had held simply that a city can't ban *all* camping at all times and in all public places. But *Martin* held that a city could not enforce a ban on camping unless "shelter" for homeless individuals was "practically available." (Enforcing these laws, in real-world terms, almost always means issuing citations. Actual prosecutions merely for sleeping in public are unheard of today.)

"None of us is blind to the undeniable suffering that the homeless endure," wrote Ninth Circuit judge Milan Smith, in his dissent in *Martin*, "and I understand the panel's impulse to help such a vulnerable population. But the Eighth Amendment is not a vehicle through which to critique public policy choices or to hamstring a local government's enforcement of its criminal code."[12] He feared that the decision would "wreak havoc on our communities" and ensure the spread of already familiar scenes such as "hypodermic needles" and "human waste appearing on sidewalks and at local playgrounds."[13] The US Supreme Court refused to review the decision.

Why ban sleeping, anyway? Is sleeping antisocial? Alone, no. But such laws are essentially prophylactic: a person who sleeps in public, as a biological need, also will perform other biological or basic human needs in public. That person will store his essential property in public. That person may erect a sidewalk-obstructing shelter in public. Or use the potent drugs on which he depends there. The point of anti-camping laws was to clarify that habitation in public

In 1968, Los Angeles declared, rather ambitiously, that a person shall not "sleep in or upon any street, sidewalk or other public way." Decades later, the law was successfully challenged by homeless persons who received citations under the law.

is simply disallowed – a clear enforceable rule – instead of resorting to the old methods of harassing the homeless by enforcing trifles like littering or destroying vegetation or loitering.

Boise's ordinance strove to make explicit the city's real concern, which went far beyond a midday doze on a park bench. It instructed officers to seek out the "indicia of camping" such as "storage of personal belongings, using tents or other temporary structures for sleeping or storage of personal belongings, carrying on cooking activities or making any fire," and so on.[14] One plaintiff, for instance, was ticketed when found at a site "littered with beer cans and other garbage" that "looked like a bike repair shop with about five working bikes and bike pieces all over the place."[15]

The *Martin* ruling was, depending on your point of view, a scandalizing judicial usurpation or a sweeping blow for the dignity of homeless residents. As a matter of pure constitutional law, it has little basis in the US Constitution. Public camping, rightly or wrongly, has been banned by cities for centuries without being called into constitutional doubt, so it is certainly suspicious to suggest that, in 2018, such bans were suddenly offensive to our Bill of Rights. For a defendant who believes that a criminal law is simply impossible for him to comply with, the law in California allowed what is called the defense of "necessity."[16] This shields the individual in the particular circumstances of that person's case – but here the court held that an entire category of law was largely unenforceable.

So far, trial court decisions after *Martin* (about a dozen as of this writing) have limited the reach of the decision. First, these rulings have suggested that *Martin* only operates to forbid a complete, exceptionless citywide ban on camping (unless shelter is available for those being displaced); cities remain free to ban camping in certain or even most areas. Second, and more important, courts have almost unanimously found that, as a decision under the cruel and unusual *punishments* clause, *Martin* only applies to criminal sanctions or the methods of criminal procedure (fines, arrests, or prosecutions) and not to official action for civil health and safety reasons. For this reason, federal district courts have upheld (1) displacements through "clear and clean" operations, or (2) demands that homeless individuals simply not camp in a particular downtown area, or (3) relocations that are otherwise forced but do not necessarily involve threat of arrest.[17]

That said, some courts have gone further; these decisions portend a federal judicialization of this uncommonly complex issue. Aberdeen, Washington (population 16,896), faced one of the first challenges under *Martin*. Members of its homeless population attacked the city's decision to evict about 100 individuals from an encampment, on city property, called "River Camp." Some had called it home for eight years. It was plagued by untreated human waste and discarded needles and was a hotspot for police calls for theft, drug use, sexual assault, and tent fires, even as the location made it difficult for first responders to arrive. It was near a railyard and a woman's legs were severed while she crawled under a train. The city prepared to clear the encampment and enforce its law against camping on public property. But a court blocked the effort, partly on grounds that the court had to "assess the city's regime more thoroughly" for compliance with *Martin*.[18] The city later settled the suit.

Another case, in Grants Pass, Oregon (population 38,191), featured three homeless individuals who alleged that the city "implemented a web of ordinances, customs, policies, and practices that, in combination, criminalize the existence of homeless people." Between 2015 and 2017, Grants Pass police allegedly issued 208 anti-sleeping and anti-camping citations, primarily to homeless individuals. The court concluded that the city had an unwritten policy of chasing away the homeless. In July 2020 it held, for the first time in a homelessness case, that the cruel and unusual punishments clause applies, "whether the punishment is designated as civil or criminal."[19] This applied *Martin* to forbid not just arrests, fines, or prosecutions, but even non-punitive measures like "move-along orders" and "warnings." The implications of that decision are immense: it forbids a city (unless it has shelter) from enforcing a citywide ban on camping, even a decriminalized ban. This effectively creates a constitutional right to be homeless, all under what seemed, a few years ago, to be the unlikely aegis of the cruel and unusual punishments clause. The facts of the case revealed how complex the issue can be. For instance, one plaintiff who received a ticket, Gloria Johnson, lived in a van while receiving $1,600 a month in benefits. Yet the city's observation that this income suggested a measure of choice about her living arrangements drew a rebuke from the court, which wrote that the city "misunderstand[s] the nature of modern homelessness."[20]

Other courts presage extensions of the *Martin* decision beyond the context of nighttime sleep. After all, if it is impermissible under the Eighth Amendment to punish people for a necessity of biology like sleep, what about other unavoidable bodily functions? A group of homeless men and women in Sacramento challenged, under *Martin*, the removal from the street of a portable toilet that two relief-minded nurses had delivered for the homeless individuals' use. US District Court judge Kimberly Mueller found that *Martin* did not *prevent* the removal of that toilet but nevertheless held that, "[e]xtending *Martin* to these facts, the City may not prosecute or otherwise penalize the plaintiffs ... for eliminating in public if there is no alternative to doing so."[21] So Sacramento had this choice: leave the toilet on the street or leave off enforcing laws against relieving oneself in public.

Sidewalk Obstruction and Sitting or Lying Down in Public

Most cities forbid the obstruction of sidewalks or other rights-of-way. The justification is the need to keep public rights-of-way accessible, especially for those who would otherwise have to veer into streets, for example, those in wheelchairs or using strollers.[22]

In 1994, New York City, under Mayor Rudy Giuliani, undertook a "Quality of Life" initiative designed to reduce a "wide range of street crimes," from prostitution to panhandling. The New York Police Department issued a guide for police, listing the laws that prohibited the sort of conduct targeted by the initiative. One such law forbade leaving boxes and erecting obstructions in public spaces. In February 1997, a homeless man named Augustine Betancourt was arrested in a lower Manhattan park (in a 1 A.M. sweep that also netted twenty-four others) when cops found him with "some personal possessions" and "three folded cardboard boxes, and a loose piece of cardboard." Using these boxes he constructed a tube, placed it on a park bench, and went to sleep.[23] The law was challenged as unconstitutionally vague, but the panel majority found that an "ordinary person would understand that an agglomeration of boxes large enough for a man to fit into would be 'something that obstructs or impedes.'"[24]

Judge Guido Calabresi dissented:

Why doesn't the law apply to a woman who, having wrapped herself in a fur coat and silk scarf, regularly reclines on a park bench to feed the birds? Or to a passing sportsman who, while awaiting his tour bus, takes a nap after lashing together his ski boots, skis, and snowboard? Or to the midnight photographer who mounts his camera onto a tripod and waits patiently for the perfect picture? Or would it apply in these situations, but only if the city administrators or the police were averse to pigeons, snowboarding, or troublesome artists?

The ordinance, he continued, was an "impenetrable law that could be read to allow police officers to apply the ordinance almost however they want against virtually whomever they choose."[25]

Other cities have drafted more targeted variations on broad street-obstruction laws. In 2016, San Francisco voters passed an ordinance for the "promotion of safe and open sidewalks." It is functionally an anti-tent law. It makes it "unlawful to place ... upon a public sidewalk ... a tent or any structure consisting of any material with a top or roof or any other upper covering or that is otherwise enclosed by sides that is of sufficient size for a person to fit underneath or inside while sitting or lying down."[26] The findings behind the measure stated:

> San Francisco is a compassionate city and must do everything possible to transition people experiencing homelessness to stable and successful permanent housing by providing services and low-barrier-to-entry shelters. But prolonging encampments in our neighborhoods does not help homeless individuals, nor does it make our neighborhoods safer.... Encampments also often exhibit the presence of syringes, feces, urine, and uncontained food, all of which present public health risks and can become vectors for disease, illness, and rodents.[27]

Separately, "sit-lie" laws arose to fill the gap that non-enforcement of broadly phrased sidewalk-obstruction laws left open, usually in cities with the most acute homeless problems, such as Los Angeles, Santa Monica, and Santa Cruz.[28] In the mid-1990s, Seattle's sit-lie law was tested against the federal Constitution – particularly the free speech clause – in *Roulette v. City of Seattle* (1996). There, the Ninth Circuit considered an Emerald City ordinance that generally prohibited individuals from sitting or lying on public sidewalks in certain commercial areas between 7 A.M. and 9 P.M.[29]

The law *allowed* sitting or lying in public parks, private or public plazas, or alleys; or sitting on the sidewalk in noncommercial areas of the city; or sitting on the sidewalks in the commercial areas at night. Plus, police had to notify the person that he or she was sitting or lying unlawfully before a ticket could issue. The court, in an opinion by Judge Alex Kozinski, rejected the assertion that merely sitting or lying on the sidewalk was a form of "expression."[30] This provoked a fierce dissent from William A. Norris, who believed that a man lying on the street *does* convey a message, one that "addresses what many consider to be the single most compelling problem facing our nation: the growing disparity between the haves and the have-nots."[31] He continued: "Thus, those deemed 'desirable' by shopkeepers may sit on the sidewalk and obstruct pedestrian traffic all day long, drinking their cappuccinos and reading their *Wall Street Journals* to their hearts' content. But someone with an unpopular political message or an unsightly beggar symbolizing the failure of our society to achieve economic justice, may not sit, even to add power and content to his message."[32]

In 1994, New York City, under Mayor Rudy Giuliani, undertook a "Quality of Life" initiative designed to reduce a "wide range of street crimes," from prostitution to panhandling. The New York Police Department issued a guide for police, listing the laws that prohibited the sort of conduct targeted by the initiative. One such law forbade leaving boxes and erecting obstructions in public spaces.

San Francisco's sit-lie law, in turn, declared that existing laws against obstruction of sidewalks failed to "address the safety hazards, disruption and deterrence to pedestrian traffic caused by persons sitting or lying on sidewalks."[33] The ordinance was passed in 2010 by Proposition L, which made it illegal "to sit or lie down upon a public sidewalk" between 7 A.M. and 11 P.M., with a number of exceptions, such as for medical emergencies or while observing a parade. Individuals receive a warning first, which, if not obeyed, can lead to a fine for the first offense. The city is also mandated to offer "social services needed by those who chronically sit or lie down on a public sidewalk."[34] The law stated in its findings that "business areas and neighborhoods become dangerous to pedestrian safety and economic vitality when individuals block the public sidewalks. This behavior causes a cycle of decline as residents and tourists go elsewhere to walk, meet, shop and dine, and residents become intimidated from using the public sidewalks in their own neighborhoods."[35]

The law also noted that the city has "offered and offers services to those engaged in sitting or lying down on the sidewalk who appear to be in need, or to those who request service assistance, but the offers are refused in many cases or people continue the conduct despite the provision of services."[36] The ordinance has critics. "The whole thing is really just a waste of time because you are just shifting people around the city," said Brian Pearlman, managing attorney for the SF Public Defender's misdemeanor unit. "If you don't have any shelter and you keep moving along, you are not going to get cited, so it's kind of silly."[37]

But this result is not so silly to, say, the businesses being undermined by the unrestricted street lounging. Merchants were always the folks most likely to summon the police. In 2013, the *San Francisco Chronicle* spoke to Haight Street storeowner Cicely Ann Hansen, who had called the police on individuals sitting and drinking in front of a business next door:

> "The Red Vic [a next-door hotel] doesn't do anything – they're hippies. They think people have human rights," said Hansen, using her fingers to put air quotes around "human rights." "I pay the rent here," she said. "I'm the one who gives the city $50,000 a year in sales tax. Where are my rights?" Hansen said she loved the Haight in the 1960s and counted Janis Joplin and the members of the Grateful Dead as friends. But she said the neighborhood isn't the same anymore and that she's tired of having clearly crazy street people scare potential shoppers away.[38]

It was Haight Street's deterioration that provoked San Francisco's sit-lie law. Passersby were menaced by roving groups of surly youths, often with short-leashed pit bulls and juiced by drugs and alcohol, making streets fearsome or unwalkable. Today Haight Street is again a shopping district.

Keeping or Storing Personal Belongings in Public

Many cities have laws that regulate the keeping of private property in public spaces. These laws, naturally, fall hardest on the homeless, who have few places other than public space in which to keep goods.

A saga respecting this type of law continues to play out in Los Angeles over the city's restriction on permissible street property. In 2012, the Ninth Circuit, in *Lavan v. City of Los Angeles*, in an opinion written by Judge Kim Wardlaw, agreed with a number of homeless plaintiffs living in the Skid Row district that the city violated their property rights under the Fourth and Fourteenth Amendments "by seizing and immediately destroying their unabandoned personal possessions, temporarily left on public sidewalks while [they] attended to necessary tasks such as eating, showering, and using restrooms."[39] Those rights, she wrote, were not lost when the plaintiffs left their property "momentarily unattended in violation of a municipal ordinance."[40] The court protested, perhaps too much, that its ruling did not "concern the power of the federal courts to constrain municipal governments from addressing the deep and pressing problem of mass homelessness or to otherwise fulfill their obligations to maintain public health and safety."[41] The dissenting judge, Consuelo Callahan, wrote,

> Although I sympathize with the plight of the homeless and believe that this is a problem that we must address as a society, a [civil rights lawsuit] is not the proper vehicle for addressing this problem. The majority opinion focuses on the interests of the homeless in Skid Row who leave their property unattended and does not acknowledge the interests of the other people in Skid Row – homeless or otherwise – who must navigate a veritable maze of biohazards and trash as they go about their daily business.[42]

Callahan noted that individuals who wished to avoid the seizure of property could have heeded the city's notice that on weekdays, between 8 A.M. and 11 A.M., city employees would gather and dispose of unattended property, and that a free public storage warehouse was available to the residents of Skid Row.[43]

A few years later, in 2016, Los Angeles moved to restrike the balance that was unsettled by *Lavan*. The city revised its law to abolish the prior policy of disallowing residents from keeping personal property on streets – in favor of a more limited policy of allowing unhoused men and women to keep possessions on public property *so long as the objects were not too numerous, dangerous, or large*. The intent was to protect the constitutional property rights of the homeless while ensuring safe, sanitary sidewalks for everyone – including the homeless. Yet US District Court judge S. James Otero effectively blocked the new compromise two days after it took effect. In a lawsuit called *Mitchell v. City of Los Angeles,* he was persuaded, at least preliminarily, that the city was violating the property rights of the homeless by cleanups that involved the indiscriminate confiscation of necessities such as blankets and medicine. Three long years later, the city settled the suit and agreed to clean up property only when the property is "abandoned, presents an immediate threat to public health or safety, is evidence of a crime, or is contraband." The settlement stipulates that the city can remove large items like couches and refrigerators from the sidewalks or remove property that prevents the disabled from passing by or entering a building.[44]

Living in Vehicles

Living in vehicles generally does not pose the same concerns as sidewalk obstruction, littering, and open drug use. Probably the most common complaint against vehicle living is the loss of parking asserted by neighbors. But it has become another arena in the larger fight over homelessness. The problem has been particularly urgent in Silicon Valley suburbs, where residents complain of large recreational vehicles dominating their street fronts. In Santa Clara County, one report found that nearly one in five homeless people lives in a vehicle.[45] Elsewhere, less obtrusively, like in San Francisco, vehicles line the highways along the beach.

Larger cities are experimenting with "safe" spaces – i.e., set-aside lots for people to park lawfully. Often they have the virtue of being lighted, surrounded by fences or security, or stationed with potable water or toilets. In San Francisco (which recently tallied some 600 passenger vehicles, RVs, or vans that were apparently inhabited) and in Oakland, "safe sites" have opened.[46] San Diego mayor Kevin Faulconer said:

> Policy makers . . . have to intervene before people end up on the streets. For some folks, their vehicles are homes of last

resort. That's why we have three sanctioned "safe" parking lots for people living out of their cars or RVs – so they can go there at night instead of parking in front of people's homes and businesses. It's a gated, safe space where they can access services, find a job, and eventually get back into homes of their own.[47]

The biggest legal fight over vehicle living arose in Los Angeles. A provision in the city's municipal code prohibited use of a vehicle "as living quarters either overnight, day-by-day, or otherwise." In 2014, the Ninth Circuit invalidated the law in *Desertrain v. City of Los Angeles*. The court, in a decision by Judge Harry Pregerson, found the law to be a "broad and cryptic" ordinance that "criminalizes innocent behavior."[48] The court recognized that Los Angeles had valid reasons to prohibit living in cars, but the "record plainly shows that some of the conduct plaintiffs were engaged in when arrested – eating, talking on the phone, or escaping the rain in their vehicles – mimics the everyday conduct of many Los Angeles residents."[49]

The record *also* made clear, it seems only fair to observe, that police were not stopping cars loaded for a camping trip or occupied by a dozing livery driver. The police knew vehicle living when they saw it. But that very fact allowed the police, in the court's view, to "target" the homeless: the law was "broad enough to cover any driver in Los Angeles who eats food or transports personal belongings in his or her vehicle. Yet it appears to be applied only to the homeless."[50] The court concluded: "For many homeless persons, their automobile may be their last major possession – the means by which they can look for work and seek social services. The City of Los Angeles has many options at its disposal to alleviate the plight and suffering of its homeless citizens. Selectively preventing the homeless and the poor from using their vehicles for activities many other citizens also conduct in their cars should not be one of those options."[51]

Living in vehicles generally does not pose the same concerns as sidewalk obstruction, littering, and open drug use. Probably the most common complaint against vehicle living is the loss of parking asserted by neighbors.

In response, Los Angeles devised a narrower ordinance that bans "dwelling" in vehicles at night in residential areas or within a block of parks, schools, and daycares.[52] "Dwelling" was defined as activities that "reasonably appear, in light of all the circumstances, that a person is using a vehicle as a place of residence or accommodation," such as "possessing" items "not associated with ordinary vehicle use," such as sleeping bags, cookware, and bodily fluids.[53]

Yet this narrower version did not placate opponents, who were concerned less with any question of constitutional vagueness than the underlying policy that the ordinance implements. The *Los Angeles Times* reported:

> At a hearing at City Hall, local activists argued that it was cruel and counterproductive to punish people for bunking down in vehicles while housing, shelters and "safe parking" programs for homeless people remain inadequate. Despite the impassioned pleas from opponents, the council voted 13-0, without any discussion, to reinstate the rules. Immediately after the vote, opponents began shouting in disbelief and anger, bringing the council meeting to a halt. Many in the crowd started chanting, "Shame on you!"
>
> As police detained one person in handcuffs and ushered other activists out of the room, Councilman Marqueece Harris-Dawson briefly spoke to reporters, calling the rules "an attempt to strike a balance." Letting people park and sleep anywhere at any time would be "totally unacceptable" for neighborhoods, Harris-Dawson said. For instance, the councilman said that RVs lined up around one park have blocked parking and stopped residents from using the park. In letters to the council, some Angelenos complained about trash and filth from cars-turned-homes.[54]

Today, across Los Angeles's 500 square miles, roughly 10,000 people live in some 5,000 vehicles.[55] Mayor Eric Garcetti says the city aims to get the total number of safe parking spaces to about 300. Meanwhile, he said, the city has homeless outreach teams working to find people in vehicles and connect them to social services. "We want to make it easier" for people living in vehicles, he said, "but we also have to have that balance... making sure that it's not going to be chaos out there."[56]

Laws Against Panhandling

Begging in public is another area of regulation tied to homelessness. Street beggars were called "mendicants" in the colonial era; today they are labeled "panhandlers." Their distinguishing quality is to seek money for their own use, not for, say, the Salvation Army. Some rely on panhandling to obtain money for food, others for fentanyl. Either way, cities regulate it on grounds that those on the receiving end of requests for money often find beggars somewhere between off-putting and menacing.

Courts allow cities to regulate panhandling – but a series of judicial decisions have narrowed their municipal authority to do so. In 1990, the US Court of Appeals for the Second Circuit, sitting in New York City, rejected a free speech challenge to the city's anti-panhandling policy by holding that "the conduct of begging and panhandling in the subway amounts to nothing less than a menace to the common good." Panhandling, the court continued, was unlike requests for donations by organized charities, since these entities "serve community interests by enhancing communication and disseminating ideas."[57]

But a year later, US District Court judge William Orrick in San Francisco, facing a similar challenge to California's general ban on panhandling, called the Second Circuit's reasoning "disturbing." Panhandling, far from being a menace, he said, was a form of *free speech*: "Begging gives the speaker an opportunity to spread his views and ideas on, among other things, the way our society treats its poor and disenfranchised."[58]

He offered his view about what he felt was *really* going on: "City authorities claim the power to remove from this public forum those that … make the rest of us uncomfortable. The speech of the needy around us may well be subjectively felt as an unwelcome intrusion by some, but the expressive freedom guaranteed by the Constitution has never been costless."[59] The decision was later vacated, but the court anticipated the legal trend.

In 1993 came the most noted case on panhandling: *Loper v. New York City Police Department*. The US Court of Appeals for the Second Circuit held that New York City could not enforce an outright city-wide ban on panhandling. The free speech clause protected panhandling, the court wrote, because "begging implicates expressive conduct or communicative activity."[60] The judges declared that the *Young* decision from three years earlier was limited to the context of panhandling on *public transportation*. The court wrote:

> Begging frequently is accompanied by speech indicating the need for food, shelter, clothing, medical care or transportation. Even without particularized speech, however, the presence of an unkempt and disheveled person holding out his or her hand or a cup to receive a donation itself conveys a message of need for support and assistance. We see little difference between those who solicit for organized charities and those who solicit for themselves in regard to the message conveyed. The former are communicating the needs of others while the latter are communicating their personal needs.[61]

The *Loper* decision encouraged cities to frame their panhandling laws in ways that more directly advance the real interest behind such laws: not banning *all* solicitation but solicitation that leaves passersby intimidated. Take Measure M, passed by San Francisco in 2004. The city announced in the law:

> The people of San Francisco find that aggressive solicitation for money in public and private places threatens residents' and visitors' safety, privacy and quality of life. San Franciscans seek policies that preserve citizens' right to enjoy public spaces free from fear and harassment while protecting the free speech rights of individuals and groups, permitting appropriate and safe commercial activities of street artisans, performers and merchants and providing for the basic needs of indigent and vulnerable populations.... [T]he city's existing laws regulating panhandling and solicitation are outdated and unenforceable as a result of numerous court decisions.[62]

San Francisco's law now forbids (1) "aggressive" solicitation in public, defined to mean solicitation that involves menacing behavior, touching, blocking, following, or overly persistent solicitation, and (2) solicitation in certain places, namely near ATMs, from people in cars, and on buses or in parking lots. Before citations or arrests, an officer has to give the individual a chance to cease the activity. A charged and convicted offender can be fined $50 or more. But he or she can also avoid the fine by attending a screening program designed by the Department of Public Health to see if drug or alcohol counseling or mental health services are appropriate.[63] As the *San Francisco Chronicle* reported at the time,

> The city intends to enforce the new law gently, using it not so much as a police tool as an opportunity to persuade homeless people to trade in their panhandling cups and signs for spots in emergency shelters or counseling programs. Instead of getting hustled off to jail by squads of cops when they're caught near ATMs or in traffic lanes - prohibited spots under the law - panhandlers are more likely to get visits from social workers. Police officers will warn panhandlers verbally about the law and will issue citations if they become belligerently persistent, but that's not the main thrust of the city's plan.[64]

In 2010, the US Court of Appeals for the Seventh Circuit, based in Chicago, upheld an Indianapolis law that, similarly, restricted only "aggressive" panhandling. The court wrote that "[l]aws targeting street begging have been around for many years, but in the last twenty years, local communities have breathed new life into old laws or passed new ones. Cities, such as Indianapolis, have tried to narrowly draw the ordinances to target the most bothersome types of street solicitations and give police another tool in the effort to make public areas, particularly downtown areas, safe and inviting."[65] The court upheld Indianapolis's limited ordinance:

> The city determined that vocal requests for money create a threatening environment or at least a nuisance for some citizens. Rather than ban all panhandling, however, the city chose to restrict it only in those circumstances where it is considered especially unwanted or bothersome - at night, around banks and sidewalk cafes, and so forth. These represent situations in

which people most likely would feel a heightened sense of fear or alarm, or might wish especially to be left alone.... [T]he city has effectively narrowed the application of the law to what is necessary to promote its legitimate interest.[66]

Cities also retain their latitude to restrict solicitations (of any kind) in places that are public yet more confined than streets, such as state fairs, subways, and airports.[67]

Yet even despite these clarifications of the law, now over decades, the issue arises perpetually, as a policy if not a legal matter, as cities struggle to balance compassion, individual rights, and order.[68] For instance, in 2019, BART, the public transportation system between San Francisco and the East Bay (e.g., Oakland, Berkeley), debated the issue:

A ban on panhandling in BART trains wouldn't violate the First Amendment, the agency's staff said in a new legal analysis that rattled an already tense debate among board directors. It's the latest development in a fight that keeps flaring up, as officials weigh the rights of people to entertain and ask for money against the rights of riders to be left alone. Supporters of panhandling restrictions say the practice intimidates and annoys commuters. Opponents fear such a law would penalize poor people and street artists, including some who create a vibrant atmosphere at BART.[69]

The legal contests over panhandling laws have led to ever more refined ordinances. In 2019, the US Court of Appeals for the Tenth Circuit, based in Denver, upheld, against a free speech clause challenge, a law in Sandy City, Utah (population 96,901), that forbids standing on any median that is "unpaved" or "less than 36 inches."[70] The city claimed that the law was designed to stop solicitation of drivers or passengers while allowing maximum freedom of expression consistent with safety. Sandy City determined that a median less than 36 inches wide was dangerously narrow to sit or stand on and that unpaved medians were inherently dangerous since they were covered with rocks or shrubs. The city was nevertheless accused by the law's challengers of contriving a "public safety justification" that is a "façade for its improper motive to suppress panhandlers' speech."[71] One dissenting judge agreed with them.

General Nuisance Laws

Ultimately, the enumeration of every danger to public health, safety, and order is impossible. Thus cities retain power to enforce general anti-nuisance laws. Many of these cover the antisocial conduct of homeless populations on the street. For instance, San Francisco's general nuisance law forbids any person from accumulating "filth, garbage, decayed or spoiled food, unsanitary debris or waste material" or "matter or material which constitutes, or is contaminated by, animal or human excrement, urine or other biological fluids."[72] But these provisions, which require formal proceedings against individuals, essentially go unenforced with respect to violations by those experiencing homelessness.

THE LIMITS OF HOUSING FIRST

Los Angeles Makes a $1.2 Billion Bet
on a Solution to Homelessness That Is Bound to Fail

8

CHRISTOPHER F. RUFO

"HOUSING FIRST" has become the political class's primary mantra on homelessness. Its basic philosophical premises can be summarized by the slogans of street protestors: "The Rent Is Too Damn High," "Housing Is a Human Right," and "Affordable Housing for All." Its inventor, Sam Tsemberis, has been lavished with praise by the national media. In 2015, the *Washington Post* wrote that Tsemberis "[has] all but solved chronic homelessness" and that his research "commands the support of most scholars."[1] As Tsemberis himself told the *Post*, "Give homes for the homeless, and you will solve chronic homelessness."

In California, where 151,278 people are homeless,[2] political leaders have gone all in on Housing First. Los Angeles mayor Eric Garcetti declared that "we need to have an entitlement to housing."[3] California governor Gavin Newsom went a step further, arguing that "doctors should be able to write prescriptions for housing the same way they do for insulin or antibiotics."[4] Cities throughout the state are scrambling to construct "permanent supportive housing" they can offer to the homeless.

However, underneath this simple rhetoric is a complex reality on homelessness, housing, addiction, and mental illness that defies the certitudes of Housing First activists. Since Tsemberis "all but solved chronic homelessness" in 2015, the number of chronically homeless individuals has actually increased 16 percent nationwide.[5] And although Housing First has been the official policy of the federal government since the George W. Bush administration, homelessness has continued to capture the streets of major American cities.

And yet, Housing First has survived as the dominant policy regime at the local, state, and federal levels. Despite Housing First's uncertainties, West Coast cities, desperate to solve homelessness, have been captured by its seductive messaging and promise of respite. The stakes are high: governments across the United States are betting billions of dollars on Housing First, while its track record has remained woefully underexamined. This chapter will explore the academic literature on Housing First and provide a counterpoint to the conventional wisdom – and determine whether those billion-dollar bets are likely to pay off.

Governments across the United States are betting billions of dollars on Housing First, while its track record has remained woefully underexamined.

Los Angeles is currently embarking on the single-largest experiment in Housing First in the nation's history. In 2016, Los Angeles voters approved Proposition HHH, a $1.2 billion bond for the construction of 10,000 units of permanent supportive housing for the homeless. The measure represents what can be termed the "housing hypothesis" – the contention that homelessness is ultimately reducible to housing and that the provision of publicly funded apartments can resolve the crisis. To support the ballot campaign, political leaders, activists, and the media constructed a simple narrative that rising rents have thrown people onto the streets and that "affordable housing" is the solution. This narrative was ultimately persuasive: when Proposition HHH went to the polls, it won approval with 77 percent of the votes.[6]

However, it appears that the campaign for Proposition HHH was the easy part. Three years later, the project has been plagued by construction delays, massive cost overruns, and accusations of corruption.[7] The Los Angeles city controller's office issued a scathing report, "The High Cost of Homeless Housing," which shows that some studio and one-bedroom apartments were costing taxpayers more than $700,000 each, with 40 percent of total costs devoted to consultants, lawyers, fees, and permitting.[8] Meanwhile, unsheltered homelessness has increased 31 percent, vastly outpacing the construction of new supportive housing units.[9] *Los Angeles* magazine, which initially supported the measure, now wonders whether it has become "a historic public housing debacle."[10]

The experience in Los Angeles reveals the limitations of the "housing hypothesis." On the practical level, which has captured much of the public outrage, the government has proven itself wasteful, inefficient, and incapable of managing large construction projects. Before completing a single housing unit, the city reduced its projected construction from 10,000 units to just 5,873 over 10 years, with the potential for further reductions in the future.[11] Even if one accepts that permanent supportive housing is the solution, there are currently more than 59,000 homeless people in Los Angeles County.[12] Under the best-case scenario, the "housing hypothesis" of Proposition HHH would solve less than 10 percent of the problem over the course of a decade.

But Los Angeles and other cities will inevitably confront a deeper challenge as their supportive housing units come online: Housing First is not the panacea that its supporters claim it to be. The "housing hypothesis" has proven to be popular in rhetorical terms but begins to break down when subjected to real-world testing. Political leaders, activists, and academics have long insisted that Housing First is an "evidence-based" intervention that reduces homelessness, saves taxpayer money, and improves lives. Supporters frequently cite that Housing First reduced costs in a study of chronic alcoholics in Seattle, consistently demonstrates high retention rates in multiple academic surveys, and eliminated chronic homelessness in Utah.[13]

Unfortunately, placed in an appropriate context, all of these arguments lose their statistical and rhetorical power. Although the study of chronic alcoholics in Seattle does show a net reduction in monthly social service costs of $2,449 per person, this figure does not include $11 million in capital and construction costs for the housing units themselves; in other words, Housing First saves money when you don't count the cost of housing.[14] Furthermore, even on its own favorable terms, the study's purported savings aren't as dramatic as they appear: while the Housing First participants showed a 63 percent reduction in service costs over six months, a waitlisted control group that was not provided housing showed a 42 percent reduction in service costs over the same time period, calling into question the causal relationship and overall effectiveness of the intervention.

Second, while it's true that many studies show one-year retention rates of roughly 80 percent for Housing First participants, this should hardly come as a surprise. When the state provides free housing, residents are highly incentivized to maintain that housing. If anything, it's surprising that retention rates aren't higher. Furthermore, even this often-cited 80 percent figure on "residential stability" is misleading.

Part II: How California Became First in Homelessness

In a meta-analysis of three best-in-class Housing First sites, researchers found that only 43 percent remained in housing for the first 12 months, 41 percent were "intermittent stayers" that left and returned, and 16 percent abandoned the program or died within the first year. Supporters argue that Housing First is a long-term solution to homelessness, but with such significant drop-off at the one-year mark, is it realistic to expect "permanent supportive housing" to be truly permanent?

Finally, advocates and the media have long touted Utah as the gold standard of Housing First. The *Daily Show* called Utah's Housing First program "mind-blowing," the *Los Angeles Times* reported that Utah "is winning the war on chronic homelessness," and dozens of media outlets announced that the state "reduced chronic homelessness by 91 percent."[15] The problem? These miraculous results were not the result of Housing First policies but part of a clerical sleight of hand by Utah state officials. According to the *Deseret News* and economist Kevin Corinth, "as much as 85 percent of Utah's touted reductions in chronic homelessness ... may have been due to changes in how the homeless were counted."[16] It's not that all of the chronically homeless were housed; they were simply transposed onto a new spreadsheet. Moreover, between 2016 and 2018, the number of unsheltered homeless in Utah nearly doubled – hardly the victory that Housing First activists had declared.[17]

Most of the recent debate over Housing First has been focused on actuarial concerns, such as cost savings and housing retention rates. This is deliberate. As a result of this shrewd market positioning, Housing First has been able to seduce Republicans and Democrats alike. The policy was first adopted by the George W. Bush administration and has been the centerpiece of the US Department of Housing and Urban Development's $2.6 billion homelessness program ever since. As the *Washington Post* observed, it is "a model so simple children could grasp it, so cost-effective fiscal hawks loved it, so socially progressive liberals praised it."[18]

But these actuarial concerns obscure a critical question that nobody is asking: What happens to the human beings in Housing First programs? Sadly, this is where the promise of Housing First completely breaks down. The results across the vast majority of studies point to a simple conclusion: Housing First does not meaningfully improve human lives.

To evaluate this contention, it's important to understand the context of unsheltered homelessness in the United States. According to research by the California Policy Lab, 75 percent of the unsheltered homeless have substance abuse conditions, 78 percent have mental health conditions, and 84 percent have physical health conditions.[19] This is a population that suffers from deep human pathologies and is in desperate need of help. In theory, Housing First would address these problems. In every program, residents are offered a wide range of services. At the Pathways to Housing program in New York, a flagship program founded by Sam Tsemberis himself, residents are served by an "interdisciplinary team of professionals that includes social workers, nurses, psychiatrists, and vocational and substance abuse counselors who are available to assist consumers seven days a week twenty-four hours a day."[20] However, despite this massive intervention, the Pathways program shows no reduction in substance abuse or psychiatric symptoms over time – in fact, those conditions often worsened.[21]

This basic finding on the human outcomes of Housing First has been replicated throughout the scientific literature. In study after study, residents of Housing First programs show no improvement regarding addiction and mental illness. They are housed but broken, wracked by the cruelest psychoses, compulsions, and torments – all under the guise of medical care. A recent Housing First experiment in Ottawa, Canada, illustrates this paradoxical outcome in stark terms.[22] Researchers divided up the study into two populations: an "intervention" group that was provided Housing First and access to primary care, medically assisted treatment, social workers, and on-demand services; and a non-intervention "control" group that was not provided housing or services – they were simply left on the streets as they were before. To the shock of the researchers, after 24 months, the non-intervention control group reported better results regarding substance abuse, mental health, quality of life, family relations, and mortality than the Housing First group. In other words, doing nothing resulted in superior human outcomes than providing Housing First with wraparound services.

Part II: How California Became First in Homelessness

How is this possible? First and foremost, Housing First programs are explicitly not oriented toward recovery, rehabilitation, and renewal. They operate on the "harm reduction" model, which allows residents to continue using drugs such as alcohol, heroin, and methamphetamine, and do not require mental health treatment as a condition of residency. In theory, this permissive policy would help "reduce harm" to the individual; in practice, however, it creates a community-level effect that makes it almost impossible for any individual to find recovery. Here is the basic chain of events: homeless individuals with substance abuse and psychiatric disorders are placed together in a residential facility where they are allowed to continue the way of life they had on the streets. Despite the availability of services, there is no incentive to use those services and no disincentive to the problematic behavior associated with street homelessness. Consequently, widespread addiction becomes the norm within Housing First programs – the worst possible environment for anyone seeking recovery.

This chain of events is not just a thought experiment. In Birmingham, Alabama, researchers inadvertently created this exact problem when they put participants of two different programs – one "recovery" program and one "harm reduction" program – in the same apartment complex.[23] Immediately after beginning the experiment, the recovery group "began abandoning the provided housing, complaining that their proximity to persons not required to remain abstinent (i.e., the other trial group) was detrimental to their recovery. They claimed that they preferred to return to homelessness rather than live near drug users." The researchers quickly stopped and reorganized the trial, and they wrote that "this unexpected reaction shows one possible risk to housing persons with active addiction."[24]

This is the paradox of Housing First: it prioritizes housing above human beings. Even in the most prestigious programs with expansive medical, therapeutic, and social-scientific resources, individuals often show a continued decline rather than a return to health. In the Ottawa study, which should cause a widespread revaluation of Housing First theory, individuals who were placed in Housing First died at a rate five times higher than individuals who were simply left on the streets.[25] This suggests an endpoint of human despair, and yet, the researchers insist that "adults who are homeless with problematic substance use can successfully be housed using a Housing First approach."

Advocates portray Housing First as a science that transcends politics, but the foundations of Housing First theory are deeply ideological. As leading researchers at the University of Alabama at Birmingham have written, "Housing First emphasizes respect for homeless individuals as consumers entitled to make choices and condemns homelessness itself as a social evil that, like slavery in the nineteenth century, should have no place in the United States today. In short, Housing First represents an important break from traditional models that focus on 'fixing' clients to make them 'housing ready.'"[26] This is a strange vocabulary: on one hand, it assumes the moral high ground in likening homelessness to chattel slavery; on the other, it reduces the homeless to "consumers entitled to make choices" in the marketplace of social services.

Neither assertion holds up to scrutiny. Housing First advocates have claimed the moral cause of abolition, but their preferred model, "harm reduction," deliberately neutralizes human values, arguing that addiction and sobriety are both morally valid choices on a spectrum of substance use. Because they are unwilling to condemn the behavior, they are forced to condemn society, and so they make the argument that "housing is a human right." But the harm reductionists miss the critical point: homelessness is a slavery of human frailty, not of human exploitation. By refusing to address the dangers of addiction in particular, harm reduction programs have prolonged human suffering and created a new form of servitude – addiction, madness, and disorder, all with the tacit blessing of the state.

First and foremost, Housing First programs are deliberately not oriented toward recovery, rehabilitation, and renewal. They operate on the "harm reduction" model, which allows residents to continue using drugs such as alcohol, heroin, and methamphetamine and does not require mental health treatment as a condition of residency.

At the same time, in a gambit of appealing to conservatives, Housing First activists have adopted the language of the free market: residents are "consumers entitled to make choices"; their success is measured under an accountant's visor. But the homeless in Housing First programs operate outside of market society; they are making choices, of course, but are exempted from any kind of reciprocity that is the definition of market exchange. They are not consumers of services, they are wards of the state – and no euphemism can change this fundamental dynamic. Ultimately, the language of the market is a cruel vocabulary; it provides residents of Housing First with the illusion of choice while failing to provide them with self-sufficiency.

But the most dangerous element of Housing First theory is its scientism. Proponents of Housing First have framed the program as "evidence-based" and scientifically supported, but they have simply replaced traditional morality with a social-scientific morality. In the end, Housing First is a descendant of positivism, which reduces man into an abstraction that can be manipulated through applied social science. As one Housing First resident told researchers, "They want to know all your problems and then they deal with everything fast. They take over the thinking process. You don't have to think about it."[27]

The evidence, however, suggests there is a limit to the positivist method. One critic of Housing First writes, "The success of positivist methods within social science relies on the ability to corral human behavior into manageable measurable constructs. As a result, social problems are decontextualized and simplified in order to generate unambiguous policy solutions."[28] In this case, the social scientists have reduced an entire gamut of human pathologies to a single variable – housing – and obstinately refused to address the deeply interconnected problems of addiction, mental illness, and spiritual brokenness.

If Housing First has achieved anything, it's this: it provides a stable residential environment for the homeless to live out their pathologies, subsidized by the federal government and administered by the social-scientific sector. The tragic result is that individuals subjected to this regime are reduced to their lowest possible potentialities. The social service providers know that the system dooms them to a lifetime of addiction, mental illness, and eventual death – yet they continue to chant the mantra that Housing First works.

In Los Angeles, political leaders are still posturing as true believers in Housing First. But uncertainty is creeping in. During the 2017 campaign, Mayor Eric Garcetti projected supreme confidence in the powers of Housing First, but he is now on the defensive, as homelessness in Los Angeles continues to increase despite billions in spending. After the federal government released a study questioning the premises of Housing First, Garcetti backed away from the unidimensional approach, telling reporters with irritation in his voice: "Sometimes people parody Housing First as 'only housing.' Nobody embraces only housing. It's got to be housing with services together."[29]

Already, the housing hypothesis is beginning to fail under the weight of its own theories. There is an emerging body of evidence that calls into question the "cost savings" of Housing First. A recent study in Massachusetts shows that Housing First does not reduce re-hospitalization and service utilization, while another study in Chicago suggests that Housing First might increase overall costs.[30] Furthermore, researchers have concluded that the purported cost savings in earlier Housing First studies would not apply to the 82 percent of the homeless population that is not chronically homeless.

This could spell disaster for Los Angeles. In the most optimistic scenario, the city will build 5,873 supportive housing units at an initial cost of $1.2 billion, plus an estimated $88 million in annual service costs associated with the Housing First model. According to the strong majority of studies, the recipients of this housing will not meaningfully improve their lives in terms of addiction, mental illness, and spiritual well-being, and there will still be 53,000 people on the streets across Los Angeles County. In other words, even by its own theoretical assumptions, Housing First is doomed to fail. It is at once an intervention too big and too small – it is too costly to scale to the crisis and too miserly in its view of human potential.

The only potential silver lining might be that the failure of Housing First will lead to a wider reckoning for the social-scientific class and its enablers in progressive politics. At the end of the Housing First experiment in Los Angeles, the city will be responsible for thousands of wards of the state with little possibility for recovery and tens of thousands of campers in its public spaces. At some point, the public will recognize the housing hypothesis for what it is: a human catastrophe, created through public policy and sold to the public under the false pretense of compassion. A few curious citizens will read through the academic literature and find a vast discrepancy between the ideological fantasies of Housing First and its real-world outcomes. They will say, "You should have known better. It was here all along."

LAWSUITS WITHOUT END

*How Courtroom Entanglement Limits
Political Solutions*

JOSEPH TARTAKOVSKY

HOMELESS INDIVIDUALS have constitutional rights to property, to safety, to due process. Courts exist to enforce these rights. But since actual prosecutions for quality-of-life offenses are almost unheard of these days, the vast majority of litigation involving these laws is made up of affirmative challenges, against the laws, subsidized by civil rights groups or law firms. These challenges have been very effective and often salutary. For one thing, these suits have forced cities and citizens to take a hard look at their policies. For another, these suits have led to the refinement of hundreds of laws, making them more effective, more constitutional, and more humane.

But reform through litigation has its dangers. Like the litigation-driven remodeling of prisons or schools, the constant recourse to courts, and to the court-made law that results, leads to judicial superintendence of the area. Sometimes that is necessary. But judicialization also poses the danger of judges, isolated in their chambers, knowing only the limited set of facts put before them by litigants, issuing sweeping decisions on a matter of immense complexity – all under the guise of "constitutional" adjudication.

Cities today continue to wrestle with homelessness. They have shown obstinacy and neglect but also compassion and creativity. Some citizens like their jurisdictions' policies; some disagree with them. That's democracy. But court decisions based on interpretations of the Bill of Rights necessarily foreclose democratic rule by declaring that a particular policy debate is *already settled* by the Constitution. If that decision reaches too far, then in fact a policy question reserved to communities, and their elected officials, is wrongly delivered to unelected lawyers and judges.

Lawsuits can be cooperative, but frequently, when they feature tense issues such as homelessness, they involve embittered parties and entrenched positions. At other times a compromise is reached between *some* plaintiffs and a city, only to find new plaintiffs kick off a new round of litigation. As US District Court judge Percy Anderson said in 2019, in ruling on a case in Southern California involving homelessness, "[w]hile trials can sometimes declare winners and losers, litigation frequently does a poor job of resolving complex societal problems."[1] Judges repeatedly indicate how much they detest being forced to confront thorny, unresolvable questions involving homelessness.

Some lawsuits have forced grand compromises. One bold experiment was the settlement between homeless-rights groups and 14 cities in Orange County in July 2019. The 51-page settlement was approved by – and, truth be told, driven by – US District Court judge David O. Carter, a decorated Vietnam veteran with a maverick reputation who has made solving the homelessness crisis a personal mission. He called the settlement an "exemplary document that the governor should know about" and a "model" for others trying to solve the homelessness phenomenon.[2] It tries comprehensively to cover key issues – provision of services, anti-camping rules, cleanups, and more. It obligates the defendant cities generally to refrain from enforcing anti-camping rules unless they provide care personnel and screening to determine appropriate placement. If an offered placement is declined, officers can give a warning, and if that is not heeded, they can enforce the anti-camping law. It allows those cited or arrested to go to "Collaborative Court." The settlement allows cleanups but requires notice to plaintiffs' counsel in certain circumstances; unsheltered people also get a 24-hour notice and the cities must provide free storage for personal property. Cities pledged to provide free clinical assessments to homeless within facilities. The settlement also set out a due process protocol for people denied shelter.[3] It all sounds promising. But will it hold? Time will tell. One risk of such settlements is that, like consent decrees, they lock in detailed policies that could well be rendered superfluous by conditions or prove unworkable. Often the decision to allow an amendment to the settlement is controlled, on one side, by activist lawyers with scant incentive to moderate.

Yet other lawsuits have spurred quick, beneficial action by cities. In May 2020, UC Hastings Law School led a suit against San Francisco after the COVID-19-caused suspension of anti-camping enforcement (among other laws) left the school's Tenderloin neighborhood, the school said, a "public health menace" that endangered everyone in the neighborhood:

> Tents [totaling around 450 in late May] were piled one on top of the other, so there was no ability for housed or unhoused residents to socially distance themselves from one another; the unhoused did not have the means to wash their hands regularly, crowds of open-air drug dealers and their customers blocked sidewalks, and needles, feces and trash littered the streets.

The city settled just over a month later. UC Hastings dean David L. Faigman reported that by the end of June, some 200 tents were gone, their residents removed to hotel rooms or safe-sleeping sites. He defended the suit against charges of "criminalizing" homelessness by emphasizing that the relocations demonstrated "dignity and respect" for the unhoused and reminding critics that living conditions for *housed* locals was also part of the calculus of justice.[4] Journalist Heather Knight wrote that it was these shuttered-in residents – "the families, the children, the immigrants, the business owners" – that were often the "unseen people of the Tenderloin."[5]

The strange and tense quality of this area of law is demonstrated in the fact that Judge Carter, while presiding over the northern Orange County settlement, was *disqualified* – a rare occurrence – from a similar case in *southern* Orange County. A suit filed in February 2019 features three homeless men (two in San Clemente and one in Irvine) and two homeless-rights organizations, together challenging the enforcement of city ordinances that allegedly allowed citations, arrest, or confiscation of property of those sleeping in public places. Three of the five defendant cities – Aliso Viejo, San Clemente, and San Juan Capistrano – sought to remove Judge Carter on grounds that, among other things, he engaged in his own fact-finding in the ongoing northern Orange County lawsuit, such as touring encampments with plaintiff organizations. The district's chief judge mandated Judge Carter's recusal, noting that Carter made statements in hearings in which he "praised the 'good mayors' who attended and 'shamed' the 'bad mayors' who did not."[6] (These "bad" mayors included defendant cities in the southern Orange County lawsuit.)

Now Judge Carter is overseeing another "collaborative" effort in Los Angeles, featuring private parties both hostile, in different ways, to the policies of the City of Los Angeles – but both seeking essentially to have Judge Carter order what they feel Los Angeles, long ago, *should* have done. On one side are businesses, schools, and other interests, outraged and injured by the disorder spilling out of Skid Row. On the other side are veteran homeless-rights activists whose general goal is to keep the city's hands off the homeless. Yet all sides seem to agree that the virtue of the suit is to call forth the power of the court to break Los Angeles's political-policy stalemate.

> *Some citizens like their jurisdictions' policies; some disagree with them. That's democracy. But court decisions based on interpretations of the Bill of Rights necessarily foreclose democratic rule by declaring that a particular policy debate is already settled by the Constitution.*

They found the right jurist. The 76-year-old Carter took to touring Skid Row to the cheers of its residents, holding free-wheeling, multi-hour hearings that "invite" city mayors to appear with solutions in hand. In March 2020, as the COVID-19 pandemic began to trigger closures, he convened a gathering packed with other federal judges, Los Angeles mayor Eric Garcetti (plus at least three other mayors), Los Angeles city attorney Michael Feuer, city council members, and activists, to which assemblage he declared: "We're going to get our elected officials back doing what they do best in this critical time. That's making good decisions on all of our part."[7]

Those "good decisions" would be prompted, the officials would soon learn, by supervisory orders from him. On May 15, 2020, he issued a remarkable, unprecedented order that required Los Angeles to relocate thousands of homeless people on account of what he called "emergency" circumstances – but circumstances that had been present for years, such as the vehicular "toxic fumes" or "potential collapse of an overpass in an earthquake" that threaten those making their abodes near freeways. Carter declared that *Martin* stood for a general right to a state-provided haven, outside the Eighth Amendment's criminal context, since the decision, he said, "gave constitutional significance to the availability of shelter." In his view, it was "cruel and unusual, in violation of the Eighth Amendment, to leave individuals experiencing homelessness no better option than to camp in hazardous areas when they have no other available shelter to enter."[8]

The Perils of Lawsuit and Settlement Cycles

Lawsuits can lead to endless sue-and-settle cycles – and frustration and stalled efforts. Take Los Angeles's ongoing saga with respect to a city law that regulates the keeping of private property on public streets. In 2016, Los Angeles, in response to demands from the homeless community, relaxed its policy on banning street property to allow unhoused people to keep their possessions on walkways – so long as the objects were not too numerous, dangerous, or large.

The city was sued nonetheless. US District Court judge S. James Otero blocked the law right after it took effect – based largely on allegations that sanitation officials were discarding the medicine and blankets of homeless individuals – even as he recognized that the city had an "important public health duty" here and lauded the city's efforts to address this complicated issue. Yet the city, instead of defending the law, took the case through an astonishing three years of "negotiations" – and then finally raised the white flag in May 2019. The city agreed to pay $645,000 to the plaintiffs and their attorneys. What did it get in return? It got permission to clean up property that is "abandoned, presents an immediate threat to public health or safety, is evidence of a crime, or is contraband," plus the authority to remove large items such as couches and refrigerators. In every other city in America, cleaning up such property is considered a city's duty, not a concession to be earned through litigation.[9]

But it didn't end there. In July 2019, *another* group of plaintiffs sued, essentially challenging Los Angeles's newly revised practice – embroiling the city in a new suit over the law on which it had just reached a resolution, or so it thought. An exasperated Mayor Eric Garcetti said, "We have to stop the decades-long cycle of hoping courtrooms will solve our homelessness crisis and our public health challenges. This dynamic has only resulted in the deterioration of conditions on the streets, even as more housing units and shelter beds are being built."[10]

Recently, the city, in its cleanup efforts, has sought a lighter, trust-building touch. This included placing out more trash bins and mobile restrooms and "embedding" outreach workers from the Los Angeles Homeless Services Authority with sanitation teams during cleanups. But months later, the *Los Angeles Times* reported, "some council members lamented that streets looked worse than before. Council President Nury Martinez said that Los Angeles must lead with compassion, but 'we also have to restore order in our streets.'" Meanwhile, a representative of KTown for All, an important Los Angeles homeless-rights group, came to the exact opposite conclusion: "In a city where three unhoused people die per day, it's irresponsible and, frankly, is life-threatening to continue these strong enforcement policies."[11]

KTown for All soon sued and, in April 2020, won a preliminary injunction against the enforcement of the provision of the public-storage ordinance allowing seizure of "bulky items." Two plaintiffs, whose pet cage and homemade carts were seized, respectively, convinced US District Court judge Dale S. Fischer that the city's destruction of these items violated their Fourth Amendment right against unlawful seizures of property and their due process clause right to a hearing before losing their property. Los Angeles, the court held, could not destroy property based on its size alone.[12]

In July 2002, the Los Angeles City Council voted, 10-4, to resume major cleanups around certain shelters. Councilman Joe Buscaino put forward the proposal, blaming the April decision for the pileup of abandoned property on sidewalks. "This is clearly junk, plain and simple," he said, adding: "All I'm asking is to simply clean up our streets. Why is that not acceptable?" According to the *Los Angeles Times*, the council's debate was "swamped with confusion over what, exactly, the city has been doing to clean up around encampments." Councilman Mike Bonin, before voting against the measure, complained, "I'm still unclear on what the hell it is that we're asking to be done."[13] He is not the only one.

When Courts Become the Vanguards of Change

Complications arise when the court becomes the vanguard of change, instead of merely confirming progress in public attitudes. Granted, it is often hard to tell which comes first, but there is a clear trend toward the judicialization of the homelessness crisis. The *Martin* case is one example. Here a federal appeals court adopted, as a matter of constitutional law, a creative but legally unsupported theory that some activists had pressed unsuccessfully for years: that to disallow people from sleeping in public, when they have no place else to go, "criminalizes" homelessness. This legal argument for years had been rejected by courts in unequivocal terms:

> › In 1994, in *Joyce v. City & County of San Francisco*, homeless plaintiffs challenged, under the Eighth Amendment, San Francisco's "Matrix" program – an offensive against various low-level street crimes – that penalized what the plaintiffs called "life-sustaining activities" (above all, sleep). The court concluded that the rule sought by the plaintiffs would "realistically have the effect of requiring the city to altogether cease enforcing the challenged criminal laws" and constitute a "revolutionary doctrinal decision." [14]

> › The district court in *Jones v. City of Los Angeles* (2004) reached the same result, holding that even if homelessness were a sort of "status," which generally cannot be punished, Los Angeles still had the power to punish *acts* such as street sleeping. [15] (Two years later, that decision was reversed by the Ninth Circuit, a decision that was itself vacated when the city settled the case.)

> › In *Lehr v. City of Sacramento*, in 2009, a suit against Sacramento over its anti-camping ordinance, the court found the Ninth Circuit decision in *Jones* (the decision later reinvigorated by the *Martin* ruling) unpersuasive and lambasted its reasoning as "tenuous at best." [16] "While this court is sympathetic to the plight of plaintiffs in this case," the judge wrote, "as well as to that of all individuals who are without shelter, a decision in favor of plaintiffs today would be dangerous bordering on irresponsible." [17]

> › In *Veterans for Peace Greater Seattle, Chapter 92 v. City of Seattle*, in 2009, a group of some 70 homeless individuals in Seattle challenged a "sweep" that closed their camp. The court found that Seattle's actions were justified by its substantial interest in "protecting public safety and promoting the economic health of its commercial areas." The Eighth Amendment, the court wrote, "very clearly does not apply." [18]

In short, a legal proposition that courts for 25 years dismissed as "revolutionary" or "irresponsible" or "clearly" inapplicable is now the law of the land in the western United States.

Judge Marsha Berzon, author of the *Martin* decision, adopted the rallying cry of homeless right activists by writing that "ordinances criminalizing sleeping in public places were never a viable solution to the homelessness problem."[19] But who claimed that "criminalizing" sleeping in public places was meant to serve as a "solution" to homelessness? Certainly Boise didn't. But such laws *are* meant to maintain order, public health, and safety. The *Martin* ruling didn't even bother to acknowledge the real and fearsome link between widespread homelessness and public health. It never even uttered the words "health" or "safety." That is unfortunate, because a person living on the streets doesn't just *sleep* there. If that person grapples with addiction, she will abuse psychoactive drugs there. If she suffers from psychosis or schizophrenia, she will have episodes there. The same sidewalks that serve as beds will double as repositories for human waste. Street camping, day after day, can produce mountains of rotting trash that breed disease-bearing rats, which in turn nourish disease-bearing fleas.[20] The court never paused to consider that these conditions cause physical harm and disease that is no less "biologically compelled" than sleep. These are the reasons, and by no means the only ones, that on average three homeless people die each day in Los Angeles County.

Regardless of the correctness of the ruling, *Martin* imposed a sweeping constitutional rule that, as written by the panel, is vague and impractical. The decision, a moral statement more than a workable rule of law, raises dozens of questions that the panel decision did not consider. That's one problem with the attempt to judicially address complex social issues.

The decision forbids enforcement of anti-camping laws unless shelter (or "alternative sleeping space") is not "practically available." No one actually responsible for the crisis of homeless habitation knows what these vague phrases mean. Does

The **Martin** *ruling didn't even bother to acknowledge the real and fearsome link between widespread homelessness and public health. It never even uttered the words "health" or "safety." That is unfortunate, because a person living on the streets doesn't just* **sleep** *there. If that person grapples with addiction, she will abuse psychoactive drugs there. If she suffers from psychosis or schizophrenia, she will have episodes there.*

"alternative sleeping space" mean publicly provided shelter or *any* alternative to street sleeping (whether a friend's house, church pew, riverside encampment, etc.)? Does it mean indoor shelter only, as opposed to set-aside camping grounds (as some cities are experimenting with on, say, urban parking lots)?

And what does "practically available" mean? For instance, one of the named plaintiffs, Robert Martin, actually had a home *elsewhere* in Idaho, but he camped in Boise when he visited friends and family there. (So could he have stayed with them?) Another plaintiff liked camping because he disliked paying rent. (So how impecunious does one have to be before renting an apartment can be effectively required?) Does it matter if the individual himself *caused* the practical unavailability? One plaintiff said that shelter was unavailable to him because he missed the time cutoff for entry. (Is he exempt from anti-camping laws merely because he failed to hasten to the shelter in time?) Another plaintiff was barred from a shelter because he violated its policies. (So can an individual contrive to get expelled from the town's shelter, then remain free to camp?) Yet another plaintiff disliked a shelter's proselytizing component. (So how much religion is too much, given that many shelters are church-affiliated?)[21] *Martin* will make these and other questions the subject of years of court proceedings. Each new decision will threaten to reduce the authority of flexible, democratically elected city councils.

The Real Harms to Be Addressed
by Policies of Getting People Off the Streets

Deon Joseph is a Los Angeles Police Department officer who patrolled Skid Row for over 22 years. He befriended and helped thousands of its residents; he also arrested hundreds of others. Joseph has become an activist for firm law enforcement while demonstrating the compassion those on Skid Row deserve. He captured the challenge perfectly:

> Most people I talk to about this issue do not hate the homeless. What they hate are the needles, used condoms, trash, sidewalk blockage, the drug usage and sales, the gangs that

are drawn to them who exploit them, the human trafficking, and lewd activity that stems from it when they become a pro-tected class that does not have to abide by rules that exist to keep us all safe.[22]

For most of American history, "vagrants" were seen as individuals with demons to be exorcized, to use historian Kenneth Kusmer's phrase, rather than luckless fellow citizens to be assisted. That no longer describes the attitudes of the majority of the public or office-holders. Most Californians feel genuine sympathy when they walk past the prone homeless man with a sheet pulled along the length of his body against the cold, or rain, or shame – a sheet that often resembles a shroud.

The circumstances that lead a person to homelessness are many. Reversing those circumstances requires different approaches. There is a small class of nomads, usually young and able to find work and exit street living when they wish, who find the itinerant life adventur-ous or convenient. (PBS once did a report on people in Silicon Valley living in vehicles and who were technically homeless. Included was a 23-year-old software engineer named Brandon making $175,000 a year who simply opted to save money by living in the back of a U-Haul truck and showering, getting three meals, and using the gym at his employer's complex.[23]) For many others, street life is the con-sequence of job loss. These people are motivated to return to a home but need housing support or income assistance. Most able-bodied and mentally healthy individuals who are homeless because of a lost job are typically rehoused within months. And a third category – the category that causes most of the public consternation and alarm and press coverage – consists of the "chronically homeless," the class whose impediments to sheltered life – usually lack of mental stability, a substance use disorder, or a combination of both – are too strong to overcome in any prolonged or successful way without serious intervention.

Leaving these people unaided strikes many as amoral for this rea-son: extended life on the streets is harsh, solitary, stressful, and short. In October 2019, the Los Angeles County Department of Public Health reported that the number of homeless deaths increased from 536 in 2013 to 1,047 in 2018, nearly doubling. This means three homeless deaths a day. Bodies are found on sidewalks, bus benches, hillsides, parking lots, riverbeds, and freeway ramps. People experiencing homelessness die on average 22 years earlier than those in the general population.

These sufferers are dying because they are mentally and physically exhausted, battered by the elements, poisoned by drugs, brutalized by criminals, unseen by doctors. They languish because of years

These sufferers are dying because they are mentally and physically exhausted, battered by the elements, poisoned by drugs, brutalized by criminals, unseen by doctors. They languish because of years without restoring sleep, because of years under the ever-present anxiety of being robbed. Many lost hope long ago.

without restoring sleep, or of years under the ever-present anxiety of being robbed. Many lost hope long ago. From 2016 to 2018, the drug overdose death rate in Los Angeles County was 26 times higher among the homeless than among the general population. Heart disease, homicide, and suicide are other leading causes of homeless deaths. This is the tragedy of street life and its countless tyrannies.[24]

From the perspectives of city officials and housed residents, the essential problem with life on the street is that homeless individuals do not simply *sleep* there. The areas in which they "sleep" are soiled by feces and urine, drug paraphernalia, dirty blankets, beer cans, discarded tents, uneaten food, and litter.[25] These make public areas unsightly, unsanitary, or dangerous and impose costs on the taxpayer to clean them up. Reno, Nevada, reported that during a span of weekly cleanups in a park along the Truckee River, between January and May 2019, crews collected 277 needles and an average of two 30-yard dumpsters a week of abandoned garbage. The cost of a typical cleanup was $7,357.[26] San Francisco budgeted a record-breaking $72.5 million in the 2020 fiscal year on street cleaning.[27]

The costs imposed by the unassisted mentally ill or addicted go well beyond large-scale janitorial duties. Sacramento tallied 250 homeless individuals who were the "top users of public resources" – jail stays, ambulance rides, emergency police responses, and addiction and mental health treatment – and found that they cost Sacramento over $11 million in 2015–2016.[28] This amounts to at least $44,000 a person on average. One man, Pete Taneyhill, required $150,000 a year. "San Francisco spends more per capita on homelessness solutions than nearly any other U.S. city – three hundred and thirty million dollars a year," reported the *New Yorker*'s Nathan Heller. "That sum reflects an eighty-five-per-cent increase from 2005 to 2015, when homelessness rose by thirteen percent."[29]

Street disorder undermines neighborhood prosperity. Take restaurants, a business traditionally reliant on foot traffic and an inviting atmosphere. They suffer from adjacent encampments. One, Montesacro, sued San Francisco to compel the removal of tents blocking its entrance and causing its business to plummet. In Hayes Valley, a restaurant called Nightbird found that outdoor seating, needed to accommodate diners in the COVID-19 era, placed diners alongside human feces and syringes. A Japanese restaurant, Hashiri, to provide patrons with "safety and peace," installed transparent domes in its outdoor space. An unsympathetic Jennifer Friedenbach, executive director of the advocacy group Coalition on Homelessness, responded that it was "often hard to tease out whether the restaurant is responding to legitimate issues or the restaurant is responding to affluent diners who feel guilty about eating expensive meals in the presence of destitute people.[30]

Las Vegas, in recently passing a new law against public camping, enumerated the interests that prompted the law: the city spends $2.7 million a year on homeless cleanup efforts; homeless street populations reduce property values by 5 to 15 percent; loitering, panhandling, encampments, and growing trash create blight and public health hazards; homeless street populations increase the perception that an area is unsafe (even though, as Las Vegas noted, the homeless are far more likely to be victims than perpetrators of crime).[31] "[S]afe streets are a necessary platform for neighborhood growth," wrote Philip J. Cook, a professor of criminal justice at Duke University. Many observe that "poverty is the mother of crime," he continued, but it is equally true that crime is the mother of poverty.[32]

PART III

WHAT CAN BE DONE TO SOLVE CALIFORNIA'S HOMELESS PROBLEM

*Innovative Ways to Reduce Homelessness
Despite Budget and Legal Constraints*

TAKING ACTION

Lessons Learned from
Local Changemakers

10

KERRY JACKSON AND WAYNE WINEGARDEN

THE HOMELESS CRISIS requires policies that will address the problem immediately, even if these solutions are provisional. All of California needs a plan that will help transition as many homeless persons as possible off the streets as soon as is practical.

There are a number of private homeless shelters in the state, as well as institutions that treat addiction and mental illness. But connecting the homeless to the shelters is not an easy task. It sometimes requires an intermediary.

This section focuses on policy, legal, and enforcement reforms that could make a difference in reducing California's homelessness.

Specifically, this chapter shares the story of many innovative, community-based efforts from around California that are proving effective in alleviating the local homeless problems. While one-size-fits-all solutions don't necessarily work when dealing with homelessness, these examples of local changemakers will hopefully inspire others to adapt their ideas and methods to work in their communities. It also includes reforms that local and state policymakers should consider in order to make significant progress helping people off the streets and cleaning up cities.

A Role for Law Enforcement

Few institutions come into contact with the homeless population more closely or more frequently than law enforcement officers. But law enforcement is limited in its capacity. According to Doug Wyllie, a San Francisco resident and law enforcement trainer writing for *Police Magazine,*

In the fight against homelessness, police have been thrust onto the front lines of a war they are ill-equipped to win. Police in America need help in solving the homeless problem. Sadly, in most places, the help they need is not forthcoming, or when help is there, it's not effective enough.... We cannot fix the problem of homelessness through enforcement actions alone. Police are the people being called to deal with the issue at a street level, but they are not the people who have the capabilities to address the root causes of chronic homelessness – the two most common being mental health issues and substance abuse.[1]

Officers can play an invaluable role in dealing with homelessness challenges in the short term, if their "front-line" knowledge is connected to the private institutions that have the knowledge and resources to help. Municipal governments play a pivotal role bridging this gap between law enforcement officers and private groups. It is not simply the responsibility of city hall, however. Institutions themselves "should be actively reaching out to law enforcement to let them know what they offer," says Wyllie.[2]

Examples of this public-private partnership are working across the country. Law enforcement has partnered with homeless-services providers in Fargo, North Dakota, to great success. When the officers on the streets encounter homeless persons who are new to them, the officers connect them with the Homeless Health Services Clinic, which offers primary health care, case management, and outreach.[3]

HOST Program

In Santa Rosa, the city's Homeless Outreach Services Team (HOST), operated by Catholic Charities, collaborates with the Santa Rosa Police Department to move the unsheltered homeless into services and housing.[4]

Kelli Kuykendall, Santa Rosa's housing and community services manager for homeless services, credits the program's "many successes" to its "ability to connect highly vulnerable individuals living on the streets with shelter and housing."

"People that would not have normally reached out for resources or stopped by the drop-in center now have access to our system of care, if they so choose," Kuykendall says. "This requires assertive engagement on behalf of HOST where they continue to engage with individuals and coordination with law enforcement. In terms of being a solution, I think HOST and street outreach in general are part of a bigger strategy to resolve homelessness that must include a continuum of services."[5]

Costa Mesa's Effort

A facilitating role goes beyond the police force as well. Local governments should also become directly involved with connecting the homeless populations with private organizations that can help. The Costa Mesa City Council in mid-January 2019 approved a plan to partner with the Lighthouse Church of the Nazarene to "expand what is an already existing inclement weather shelter into a high-security temporary solution to offer shelter beds to those in need," according to the city.[6] By September 2019, more than 130 had received services at the shelter; 18 had been placed in permanent housing throughout Orange County.[7]

Reuniting Homeless with Families

Police officers are also well situated to facilitate reunifications, in which they reconnect the homeless with their families or with those who were previously providing them services. A report from the California Police Chiefs Association says, "Santa Barbara, Santa Monica, and other agencies have been successful in reuniting families using this approach." The Anaheim Police Department "also works toward reunification and utilizes a non-profit to fund the transportation costs. The non-profit then conducts the follow up with the client to insure a successful transition and alleviate the police department resources." Research shows family connections are successful in preventing individuals from returning to homelessness.[8]

Immediate Shelter

Providing temporary shelter as a means to transition the homeless off the streets is a necessary, but insufficient, service. Temporary shelter can take many forms. San Diego uses large tents that serve as transitional housing for several hundred clients in order to satisfy urgent needs. These shelters house about 700 people a night and cost roughly $11.3 million a year.[9] It is the type of transitional housing that could help people move off of the street right away.

Since transitioning homeless populations into these temporary shelters will mean that fewer funds will be needed for sanitation, temporary tents can be financed by reallocating a city's street-cleaning budget. To get an idea of how much it costs to keep a city overwhelmed by homelessness at least relatively fresh, consider that San Francisco spent roughly $54 million in the 2017–2018 fiscal year on street sanitation, a $19 million increase over 2016–2017, due to "one of the worst homelessness crises in the country," according to *Business Insider*.[10] In 2019, the city spent $94 million, "about $257,534 a day," says the *San Francisco Chronicle*, trying to keep a handle on the filth.[11] Clearly, it is a better use of the city's scarce funds to increase the availability of temporary shelters than to spend the funds on cleaning up problems created by homelessness.

Local governments should also become directly involved with connecting the homeless populations with private organizations that can help.

While fulfilling the immediate need for shelter is important, it is only the first step toward sustainably solving this crisis. Policymakers must increase their focus on establishing permanent housing once many of the people currently sleeping on the streets are housed in shelters. They can help expedite this strategy by streamlining the building permit and building code approval processes. Freeing developers from the encumbering statutes, ordinances, and regulations that discourage building lessens the need for government-managed affordable housing programs. The Legislative Analyst's Office says that "building new housing indirectly adds to the supply of housing at the lower end of the market" even though "new market-rate housing typically is targeted at higher-income households."[12]

Private-Sector Solutions

There is a long history of private-sector success in overcoming homelessness. Private organizations are typically better equipped than the government to make real differences in the lives of the homeless. They can tailor programs to specific needs and can adapt where government cannot. University of Tennessee researcher Mindy Nakamura has observed that the private sector moves faster than government, as the politics of the policymaking process "slow down decisions."[13] When discussing the advantages of state and local public services over federal efforts, President Barack Obama acknowledged that "nonprofits, faith-based and community organizations, and the private and philanthropic sectors are responsible for some of the best thinking, innovation, and evidence based approaches to ending homelessness."[14]

Andy Helmer, CEO of Vienna, Virginia–based nonprofit Shelters to Shutters, insists that "robust partnerships between private businesses and non-profits" are central to the solution for homelessness. "These partnerships," he says, "also need to be about more than just housing or just job placement. The solution truly needs to be about both."[15]

Helmer's organization has worked with apartment management companies in Nashville "to place people experiencing situational homelessness in onsite, entry-level jobs and provide them with housing at the same communities at which they work."[16]

While staying in a shelter after being evicted from her North Carolina home, Odessa Moore was introduced to Shelters to Shutters. Through the program she secured an interview for a leasing agent position at one of the apartment complexes that partnered with the organization.

She was hired, CNN said in a June 2018 report, and eventually became an assistant manager at another complex. But for Moore, there was more than just a job involved. Before participating in the Shelters to Shutters program, she had been looking for "some reason to keep my head up."[17] Gaining employment allowed her to regain dignity and feel like "Wonder Woman."[18]

Nakamura studied the work of the Crossroads Welcome Center, a nonprofit organization in Knoxville, Tennessee. She found it to be "a safe place and a starting point for people who are homeless and need a place to stay during the day, as well as a hub where the needy can come and be assessed and get in contact with the correct organizations to help them."[19]

Crossroads offers bag storage, transportation, email and internet access, and a sitting room, and it performs triage to assess personal circumstances to determine how urgent clients' problems are. It also writes referral letters that often result in additional private-sector services.[20] "If not for a day room service like this one, there would be an extra 200 people out on the streets every day," says Nakamura, who believes the "Crossroads business model can be adapted and replicated in any city across the country."[21]

Given the success private-sector institutions have achieved, as well as their advantages over public services, city officials, both elected and unelected, should do all they can to support, encourage, and expand the private sector's role in eliminating homelessness.

Addressing California's Unaffordability Problem

The strong connection between California's high cost of living and the state's homeless crisis means that sustainably addressing the problem requires reforms that restore affordability across the state. If a high cost of living were intrinsic to living in California, then the necessary policy response would be different. However, California's unaffordability is caused by the unintended consequences of policy choices that the state has made. What makes matters worse is the lack of evidence demonstrating that the policies driving California's unaffordability achieve their intended goals, let alone that achieving these goals are worth the high costs of the policies.

There are a number of examples. Burdensome restrictions created by planning commissions, zoning adjustment boards, and architectural design boards limit where new homes can be built and unnecessarily increase construction costs. The combined impact of these regulations is to restrict supply. Consequently, onerous zoning regulations are often cited as a primary factor behind California's housing unaffordability problem.

Another component is CEQA, the California Environmental Quality Act. It creates an additional set of regulatory burdens that must be managed before new construction can be built. CEQA rules are infamously inefficient, significantly restrict the supply of housing, and meaningfully increase the costs of building.

Unfortunately, housing regulations are not alone in fueling California's unaffordability problem. Electricity and gasoline costs in the state are around 40 to 60 percent more expensive than the national average due to regulations such as cap-and-trade guidelines that apply to approximately 85 percent of total greenhouse gas emissions in California; renewable portfolio mandates that require California to generate 100 percent of its electricity from zero-emission energy sources by 2045; and the recently created mandate that requires all newly constructed homes in California to have a solar photovoltaic system as an electricity source.

These regulations increase the cost of energy, which is not only an essential consumer commodity but a necessary input into the production of most other goods and services. This framework produces higher prices for goods and services across California's economy. These excessive costs are particularly taxing for the lowest-income residents, who are most at risk of falling into homelessness.

Resolving the affordability problem by implementing regulation reforms can lessen these policy-created cost problems and alleviate many of the economic pressures that drive people into homelessness. As such, these reforms are an important piece in sustainably resolving California's unique homelessness crisis.

Institutional Treatment

Once common, institutions for the mentally ill are no longer a part of our society. We have deinstitutionalized. But the cruelty and shame that had been associated with mental hospitals are with us still, just in a different form. Our co-author Christopher F. Rufo writes that the closure of institutions treating the mentally ill have produced an "invisible asylum," made up of "the street, the jail, and the emergency room."

"Slaying the old monster of the state asylums," he believes, has "created a new monster in its shadow: one that maintains the appearance of freedom, but condemns a large population of the mentally ill to a life of misery."[22]

Fifty years ago, says Rufo, many of the people we see on the streets today would have been institutionalized rather than being bounced between jail and the streets.

Rufo's observation is supported by research, which found that as recently as 40 years ago, the unintended consequences of moving patients out of institutions were beginning to be found on the streets and in public shelters.[23]

Forcing the mentally ill, who make up more than three-fourths of the unsheltered homeless population,[24] into institutions against their will is an idea that rankles many. But dismissing institutionalization entirely would be a mistake.

Rufo has documented the progression of a homeless male who was pressured to take an institutional pathway through a series of events that included "a hospital ward, an evaluation center, a jail term, two treatment programs, a halfway house, a street intervention, and a warrant hearing." The man, who suffers from bipolar disorder and multiple addictions, eventually sobered up, left the streets, and acknowledged "treatment was necessary" even if he felt like he was forced to participate against his will. "Perhaps what's needed more than anything is a renewed theoretical defense of the principles of safety, rest, morality, and health," a therapeutic track that has been "demolished" over the last half century, says Rufo.[25]

"It is a moral scandal that our society, which has surpassed the material wealth of the 19th century sixteen-fold, cannot provide an adequate sanctuary for" those with profound mental disabilities.[26]

If a high cost of living were intrinsic to living in California, then the necessary policy response would be different. However, California's unaffordability is caused by the unintended consequences of policy choices that the state has made.

Manhattan Institute fellow Howard Husock has suggested a similar approach, since "too often" this discussion about homelessness "ignores the needs of a large percentage of people living on the streets who are not capable of living independently because they suffer from serious mental health problems. For some, the best form of help may be a back-to-the-future approach: state mental hospitals dedicated to serving this particular population."[27]

Husock has not suggested a "revival of the sprawling and often poorly run system of public mental hospitals, or asylums," which in another era were "among the largest budget items of every state government." He instead proposes "safe, sanitary and clinically effective" facilities which can be "part of the tool kit for addressing the current epidemic of street homelessness."[28]

Involuntary institutional commitment might seem like a callous act, especially when it's done in large numbers. But is it truly humane to allow people to waste away and pose a threat to others? Policymakers would be more negligent than they already have been if they dismiss this option, which has more support than one might imagine, without thoughtful examination.

Policy Reforms

While private-sector charities are better positioned to directly help the homeless, policy changes are also required. Elected officials should consider an all-of-the-above approach. This could include the following steps:

Engaging law enforcement. Policies should enable law enforcement to connect homeless persons with the public and private organizations that can help transition them to permanent residences.

Expanding shelters. Policies should focus on creating shelter programs that work, such as San Diego's large tent program or Santa Rosa's HOST program. These programs can be financed by reallocating expenditures from cleaning up the streets to these expanded shelter programs.

Speeding up the housing permit process. San Francisco mayor London Breed has pledged to streamline the administration of building permits. The goal is to cut the time by half. This needs to be pursued as aggressively as possible both at the state level and in cities across California.

Embracing private-sector solutions. Programs that empower private charities or reunite homeless people with their families have had great success transitioning people off of the street and should be leveraged by policymakers.

Part III: What Can Be Done to Solve California's Homeless Problem

Publishing a comprehensive report on program and provider quality. Stephen Eide of the Manhattan Institute believes that we should be able to openly debate the merits of homeless-services programs and providers. "Not all providers are equal," he writes. They should be evaluated by "how well their education and jobs programs work and how compliant their substance-addicted and mentally ill clients are with treatment regimens." [29]

Involuntary institutional commitment might seem like a callous act, especially when it's done in large numbers. But is it truly humane to allow people to waste away and pose a threat to others?

Determining what works and what doesn't. Whenever public resources are used on the homeless, every dollar spent must be tracked so that its efficacy can be properly weighed. Providers should be judged on the number of people that move on to become self-sufficient members of the community, rather than the increasing numbers of homeless they serve.

Eliminating rent control. This would ignite a mini building boom, increase the housing stock, and push down costs.

Reforming zoning laws. Restoring the profit motive for builders in a market where the demand is enormously high would also set off an explosion of development. This includes moving to an "as-of-right" system in which the bureaucracy cannot block a project as long as it meets all zoning requirements.

Considering the Minnesota solution. The Minneapolis City Council adopted in late 2018 an ordinance that allows developers to build duplexes and triplexes in neighborhoods previously zoned only for single-family homes. It is the first major city to pass this type of ordinance.

Overhauling CEQA. This state law is the biggest barrier to homebuilding in California and significantly increases the time and costs it takes to develop new housing. CEQA reforms should focus on reducing the cost of complying with these regulations and minimizing the time delays associated with the review process. Specific reforms should include requiring the plaintiffs in CEQA lawsuits to disclose their economic interests; establishing a more certain CEQA timeline; eliminating duplicative CEQA reviews; eliminating the automatic right of appeal for non-meritorious cases; reducing the time frame in which claimants can raise issues with respect to an environmental impact report; and codifying a "harmless error" standard that prevents project denials based on minor deficiencies that would likely not impact the approval.

Embracing granny flats. Building smaller second houses on lots where homes already exist will boost the housing stock.

Supporting tiny homes. Small houses about the size of a parking space grouped together are a better option than tent encampments. This step would foster a YIMBY (yes in my back yard) attitude. Adopting this mindset would allow Californians to express their tolerance and compassion.

At the same time, state leaders need to reconsider policies and attitudes that enable and increase homelessness. They should think in terms of dignity rather than dependency and realize that massive expenditures of public funds have failed to solve the crisis.

11 SMARTER LAWS, SMARTER ENFORCEMENT

Legal and Policy Reforms to Relieve Homelessness with Humanity and Fairness

JOSEPH TARTAKOVSKY

ALL LAWS REGULATING the conduct of the homeless reflect an unavoidable tension between the rights of the few and unfortunate and the rights of everyone else in the community. Courts apply the centuries-old generalities of the Constitution to specific modern ordinances, but barely beneath the surface is a contest of visions over the proper treatment of the class of fellow residents – neighbors, even – known as the homeless. The rules in this area emerge from a trial-and-error process of reframing laws in order to strike the right balance – to safeguard the public interest while honoring the constitutional rights of those without homes.

The basic sin of the laws regulating homelessness in past eras was that they were vague catchalls that required know-it-when-you-see-it enforcement. First there were sweeping vagrancy laws, and when these came under attack, it was public drunkenness or "disorderly conduct." The real crime was usually something else that created a public disturbance: sleeping in a doorway or on a sidewalk, urinating in public, prostitution, ignoring traffic signals when crossing a street.[1]

The right way to frame laws is to address them to specific, concrete harms. This means laws against *acts* that courts recognize as antisocial. These laws are not "solutions" to the homelessness crisis. They are not meant to be. They are designed to solve immediate problems: intoxicated men sprawling in front of storefronts; the littering of blood-stained needles; tents forcing would-be patrons of sidewalk cafes to walk on; aggressive panhandling near hotel ATMs; piling up of flammable bedding in alleyways. These laws preserve the quality of life for residents of a city and the city's visitors. Of course more housing is needed. Of course more mental health services are necessary. But cities have urgent, ongoing, and unignorable health, safety, and public-order needs to address.[2]

Amend Laws to Make Them Fairer
and Less Subject to Legal Challenge

Laws can be updated and improved consistent with certain general principles.

Be precise: The laws that best balance the rights of the homeless and the rights of everyone else are those that delineate specific prohibited conduct: no camping after 8 P.M., for instance, or allowing camping in this area but not that area. That said, some measure of enforcement of quality of life laws must remain left to the discretion of peace officers, responsibly exercised.

Many court decisions involve a law being declared unconstitutional not because its *ends* were illegitimate but because overbroad drafting left it vulnerable to constitutional attack. For instance, in 1995, US District Court judge Constance Baker Motley in Manhattan struck down an Amtrak rule, as unconstitutionally vague, that permitted patrons to use Penn Station for "traveling through the station, from one point to another." The court said that this failed to "define how much time is too much time for a person to spend walking around the Station."[3] Amtrak *should* have framed the law to distinguish between individuals there with actual travel plans and those there without travel plans. This fairly distinguishes between those napping during a delay between trips and those who are using the station as a shelter. This, for instance, is how San Francisco International Airport handles it today. The police officer in charge of security at the airport reported that "every single night" a group of 20 to 30 people rides a train into the airport to sleep there for the night. So the airport's policy allows only ticket-holders to be in the airport after 10 P.M. and before 6 A.M. (All the same, police, before rebuffing the nightly visitors, provide them with addresses for places with shelter or food and bus tokens to get there.)[4]

Be candid about the real harm the law is addressed to: Cities should avoid the use of petty misdeeds in pretextual or inconsistent ways to address a pressing health and safety problem. For instance, don't use a littering law in place of anti-camping laws (unless everyone is dinged for littering). Focusing enforcement on the real problem also helps promote evenhanded application. Arkansas, for example, banned "lingering" on a sidewalk in "harassing or threatening manner" or "[u]nder circumstances that create a traffic hazard or impediment." But the fatal flaw – the reason that the law was partially invalidated by the Eighth Circuit in 2019 – was that it only applied to when such lingering was done "for the purpose of asking for anything as charity or a gift." It did not apply to those "soliciting votes, seeking signatures for a petition, or selling something," all of which could be equally harassing or problematic for traffic.[5] Laws should generally forbid a certain activity regardless of whether the person engaging in it happens to be disheveled.

Create a record of real harms behind every law: Cities and their lawyers live in an era where laws are subjected to constant constitutional attack - on theories of vagueness, discriminatory enforcement, free speech, illegal property seizure, due process, cruel and unusual punishment – and so they must prepare to defend their ordinances by creating a vivid, fact-heavy record of the concrete harms that the law is designed to prevent. This way cities defend their laws on the basis of documented necessity and avoid putting courts in a position they dislike being in – being forced to balance mere convenience or purely aesthetic concerns against the basic property rights or even life-and-death scenarios for the few.

Let the hand of the law be gentle: Laws in this area should be designed not to punish offenders but to authorize officials to solve an immediate health or safety problem and, secondarily, to deter future violations. Civil fines for disobedience or repeat offenses, if any, should be symbolic (especially since they're almost never paid anyway) and not lead to buildups of pointless warrants. They should require police to give warnings for voluntary compliance first before detaining, arresting, or ticketing. A fine can be made expungable if the individual visits services for an assessment.[6] Police must enforce quality of life laws intelligently and humanely. Finally, certainty of consequences is more important than severity.[7] This means that laws should be enforced with regularity, not haphazardly.

An old case illustrates the approach of the past and its flaws: In summer 1990, the City of Santa Ana ordered a sweep of its civic center area. Officers descended on the homeless, arresting left and right for offenses like "blocking passageways, drinking in public, urinating in public, jaywalking, destroying vegetation, riding bicycles on the sidewalk, glue sniffing, removing trash from a bin, and violating the fire code." "Some conduct," the court noted, "involved nothing more than dropping a match, leaf, or piece of paper, or jaywalking. The arrestees were handcuffed and taken to an athletic field where they were booked,

> **The right way to frame laws is to address them to specific, concrete harms. This means laws against acts that courts recognize as antisocial.**

chained to benches, marked with numbers, and held for up to six hours, after which they were released at a different location." The city was really concerned with camping. But the heavy-handed approach sat poorly with the appellate court. And it was unnecessary, because two years later, Santa Ana passed a law against camping that the California Supreme Court approved in its decision. The justices explained that they were "not insensitive to the importance of the larger issues," nor to the "disturbing nature" of Santa Ana's sweep years earlier, but ruled that "a city not only has the power to keep its streets and other public property open and available for the purpose to which they are dedicated, it has a duty to do so."[8]

Mass arrests are too authoritarian. But doing nothing is too anarchic. San Francisco's Supervisors (the city council) return from trips and remark on how the experience reveals the error of their ultra-permissive approach. Supervisor Matt Haney said he was surprised to see so few homeless people on a recent journey to Puerto Rico. "San Francisco is shocking for the level of normalcy of homelessness in the sense that people just take it for granted as a part of life here." Supervisor Rafael Mandelman added that San Francisco's live-and-let-live mentality was unlike most other cities, which "have a lower tolerance for this level of disorder," adding, "Collectively, we seem to be resistant to intervening in folks' lives." Supervisor Catherine Stefani said that "what we end up with is the status quo of allowing people to live and die on our streets." A single fact sums it up: more sleep on San Francisco's streets than on the streets in all of Britain (some 5,096).[9]

Explore the Creation of "Collaborative" or "Community" Courts

Some large cities have established programs to divert people with citations or arrests for certain "low-level" crimes into what are called "collaborative" or "community" courts. The notion is that no city has the will or resources to prosecute even a majority of quality-of-life crimes, and in any event prosecutions or jail time do little to prevent recurrence, yet they cost the city tremendously and harm those jailed. So cities might as well redirect the money received by police and jails to judges, social workers, or clinics that deliver help, not criminal sentences, and do so quickly, instead of after drawn-out proceedings. The ultimate goal is to reduce the offense rate.[10]

The original model is the Midtown Community Court (MCC) in New York City. Started in 1993, the MCC pioneered a mode of dealing with nuisance-level crime (like prostitution or fare evasion) as a "problem-solving court" that provides alternatives to fines and jail in the form of a more socially useful sentence – like serving on a cleanup crew – while connecting the individual with social services or work training. When these programs work, they can reduce recidivism (and thereby relieve police of significant enforcement burdens) and contribute hundreds of thousands of dollars of service to the community.[11]

The Community Justice Center in San Francisco, first proposed by Mayor Gavin Newsom after a visit to New York City, is a joint operation of city agencies and community groups that merges "courtroom and social-service center" by including drug treatment, mental health programs, support groups, counseling, career development, and job training. The idea is, again, to stop "cycles of recidivism while improving the lives of participants and residents in the community."[12] Judge Braden C. Woods, a former prosecutor who became a judge of that court, explained that 20 days of jail time does nothing to stop a person who stole perfume from reoffending.[13] He hears about 100 cases a day, including misdemeanors and nonviolent felonies, like drug dealing and car break-ins. Defendants are assigned a case manager and ordered to participate in anything from Narcotics Anonymous meetings to job training to mental health counseling. A 2014 story in the *San Francisco Chronicle* reported that "more than half of those ordered to appear at the court are addicted to drugs or alcohol" and "[m]ost are unemployed and lack permanent housing."[14]

Strive to Connect People to Services

A compassionate and effective approach must look at every opportunity to connect people to services. "Services" means the gamut of assistance: supportive housing, substance abuse services, public conservators, outpatient mental health counseling, check-ins by social workers, psychiatric or psychological services, vocational help, and family support. Services try to help a person address the underlying causes of homelessness, whether drugs, financial need, mental health issues, or some combination of them all. Many entered the streets because of some external event, like a lost job or work accident or ill-advised painkiller prescription; many, likewise, cannot exit those streets without an external event, namely help.

Sacramento County last year claimed success in permanently housing 209 of its 250 "costliest and most vulnerable homeless individuals." The Sacramento Steps Forward program provided wraparound social services but also housing. The key insight of the success, said Ben Avey, a spokesman for a nonprofit partner agency, was that many homeless "do not have the ability to get other aspects of their life in order until they have a bed to sleep in and a door to lock. Once you're safe and warm, and you'll be safe and warm for an extended period of time, a lot of things that may have seemed unimaginable may seem possible."[15] The program involves case workers who track down clients and get them "counseling, schooling, job training, driver's licenses and whatever else might be necessary to solve the complex problems that led them to the streets."[16]

There are limits to the salvation we can expect from services. Society cannot arrest its way out of homelessness, but it cannot spend its way out either. The promise is that services, effectively administered, at least offer a person a chance to escape the streets in ways that tickets and jail do not. The ultimate success of services in aiding a person turns on that person's voluntary desire for change.

Couple Enforcement with Outreach and Case Workers

One of the most promising ways to connect people to services is front-line "outreach" teams. Carson City, Nevada (population 55,274), has Mobile Outreach Safety Teams (MOST), partnerships that began in 2014 (and earlier elsewhere in the region) between law enforcement and mental health workers. The latter ride along with officers, often in bulletproof vests, and assist in assessing or de-escalating incidents involving mental illness. Carson City gets about 2,000 calls for responses a month and one law officer there estimated that about 60 percent have a mental health nexus.[17]

The notion behind the MOST program, according to Deputy Dean Williams in Carson City, was that "instead of just having a cop with good intentions who has had 40 hours of training, let's put the cop with someone who really knows what's going on, a licensed clinical social worker." The social worker carries a cell phone to be reachable at all times. She can ensure that medication is taken, defuse a difficult situation, and simply provide a warm human connection to people short on them. She knows individuals' stories and whether they have family that should be contacted. "The jails are not designed to handle these kinds of people, so it's nice to be able to help them so they don't go to jail," said Deputy Israel Loyola. "It helps out the jail too, because a lot of times they wouldn't know what to do with [the mentally ill]. They would put them in a cell and say 'well what do we do with them now?'"[18]

The program is most effective with unstable people who are not engaged in crime but who are creating disturbances. Social worker assistance relieves police from being mental health providers, a situation most police resent. "Strictly having police officers deal with this issue is a recipe for disaster," said Brian Marvel, president of the Police Officers Research Association of California. "This [issue] needs to be discussed from a team perspective and not dumped in the lap of law enforcement."[19] The San Francisco Police Department said that in 2019 it received "over 21,000 mental health crisis calls," nearly 60 a day on average.[20]

Mass arrests are too authoritarian. But doing nothing is too anarchic.

In Reno, Nevada, in 2011, 75 percent of contacts made by its MOST program involved a person unconnected to mental health services at the time of the initial contact. The City of Reno found that when "MOST clinicians and their law enforcement associates get someone connected to service[s], they are potentially preventing tragedy later." The Reno MOST program averages 75 to 125 contacts with individuals monthly.[21]

Clinician or social worker ridealongs also provide a sort of free training to officers in recognizing mental health issues. More broadly yet, cities might explore dispatching social workers, alone, to certain mental health calls, without the sometimes escalating presence of an armed officer.

These sorts of programs save taxpayers money because in most communities, it is the "super utilizers" – the individuals who get arrested time and again or require the most frequent ER visits – that are most helped. In Carson City, Nevada, these were essentially 10 people. One woman had been arrested or picked up 58 times in about 13 years for things like public drunkenness, throwing food in restaurants, being found unconscious on sidewalks, and, eventually, hallucinations and dementia. But under the new approach, a psychologist became her guardian, a hospital treated her dementia, and the state got her into a nursing home. The arrests and 911 calls stopped.[22]

In November 2019, the actress Kirstie Alley posted on Twitter: "Was in San Fran in Starbucks. A drunk street guy ran in screaming (it was terrifying) he began grabbing sandwiches & anything he could steal & ran out. I asked the [Starbucks] girl to call the police. She said he does it 4 times a day."[23] What would happen if, instead of an ineffectual, resource-draining police intervention here – which police evidently are unwilling to undertake in any event – it was a social worker, equipped with food vouchers, who took the call and learned the man's name and history and began to assess options?

Costa Mesa, California, implemented what it calls the "Network for Homeless Solutions," by which the city is "[i]ntegrating mental health outreach and law enforcement with a legal strategy designed to assist those seeking mental health services and housing while prosecuting chronic offenders who are resistant to help." The city enforces its rules against camping and storing of property in public, while simultaneously deploying two "community outreach workers" dedicated to serving Costa Mesa's homeless residents. Costa Mesa also created a "Psychiatric Evaluation and Response Team" to assist police by "providing on-site mental health and outreach services." In 2018, city officials, volunteers, and others spent some 1,700 hours linking homeless to legal or social services or getting individuals

IDs or rides to shelter, medical appointments, or substance abuse sessions.

Honolulu, Hawaii, likewise instituted a program to "team" police officers with social workers. "The idea is to take homeless people who are at risk for a citation or low-level arrest – such as violations of the city's 'sit-lie' ban," reported the *Honolulu Star Advertiser*, "and offer them immediate assistance through a social service agency." "Law enforcement is the portal of entry," said Heather Lusk, who helps run the programs, called Health Efficiency and Long-term Partnerships (H.E.L.P.) and Law Enforcement Assisted Diversion (LEAD). Homeless individuals with outstanding warrants are referred to Honolulu's Community Outreach Court, which "waives sometimes dozens of arrests, citations and warrants for homeless people who also agree to work with social service agencies." Lusk told the *Star Advertiser*, "Twenty are now sheltered, four completed substance abuse treatment and for one person it's the first time they've been sober in 25 years. Over 30 needed to get their IDs. At least 10 people needed legal help, such as meeting with their probation officers before going to court. We've had a couple reunified with their children."[24] Meanwhile, Honolulu Police Department captain Mike Lambert said that the partnerships with service agencies "improved morale for beat officers" because they have a "new tool" beyond arrest.[25]

San Diego is a rare large California city that has actually seen its homelessness population decline. In 2018, San Diego implemented a dual strategy of "outreach" and "enforcement." First, it created a Neighborhood Policing Division to address "quality of life" issues. This means the sort of "nuisance" crime most commonly associated with homeless individuals: public drug or alcohol use, public intoxication, graffiti, bike thefts, vehicle break-ins, aggressive behavior, and public urination and defecation. This enforcement division handles the calls from neighbors and businesses. Officers are instructed generally to offer warnings the first two times that they respond to an individual. A citation may be issued on the third encounter; the fourth run-in may end in arrest. Meanwhile, Homeless Outreach and Psychiatric Emergency Response teams work to connect the homeless with services (e.g., shelter, hepatitis A vaccinations, mental health or substance abuse treatment, medical aid). These various efforts all fall under one chain of command.[26]

San Diego Police Department assistant chief Paul Connelly told the *Times of San Diego* in April 2018 that many homeless initially decline services, but added: "'The way to overcome that is by continuing to contact the same individuals over and over again to build those trust-based relationships.... Once that trust is formed, we see people experiencing homelessness are more willing to try or accept services.'"[27] Mayor Kevin Faulconer explained:

> Sometimes you have to force people make a change. Some folks say it's not compassionate to move a homeless person off the street. I say it's not compassionate to let people die on it.... California, as a state, needs to decide that it's not acceptable to condone living outdoors in urban areas. It's not compassionate to enable the brutal life found in tent cities. It's not responsible to turn a blind eye to drug abuse. And it's not humane to let people with severe mental illness wander the streets without effective treatment.[28]

Treatment for Substance Use Disorders

Most root causes of homelessness have changed little since the colonial era. A "hobo jungle" at a train depot around, say, 1890, would have featured the same poverty, alcoholism, and mental illness that exists today. But one circumstance that seems genuinely new is the sheer power of today's drugs. Few until relatively recently had access to cheap foreign-made synthetic fentanyl, an opioid fifty times more potent than heroin. A pinch of fentanyl the size of a grain of rice can kill a non-using adult; heavy users can require intake every few hours to avoid withdrawal pain.[29] Or take methamphetamines: San Francisco Public Health director Barbara Garcia reported in 2018 that more than 50 percent of those leaving the psychiatric emergency wing at San Francisco General Hospital are under the influence of meth, a stimulant notorious for the way in which it provokes behavior – screaming, scratching, disrobing – that is hard to distinguish from mental illness.[30]

One formerly homeless man in San Francisco's Tenderloin, Tom Wolf, now a city advisor, told the *San Francisco Chronicle* that "9 out of

10 people he met living on the streets of the Tenderloin and South of Market are addicted to drugs or alcohol. He said many of them get free meals from soup kitchens so they're able to spend just about all of their general assistance checks on drugs. He said liquor stores in the Tenderloin even offer 'happy meals' – $3 crack pipes and other drug paraphernalia kept in brown bags under the counter."[31] Any serious plan to mitigate homelessness must confront the problem of substance abuse. Yet officials are often strangely reticent on the issue. California governor Gavin Newsom's February 2020 State of the State address, dedicated to homelessness, used the word "housing" 35 times but the words "drug" and "addiction" twice.[32]

Grapple with the Special Case of Encampments

Encampments – semipermanent tent communities – are the most visible and dangerous manifestation of the homelessness crisis. Encampments threaten those outside as well as those inside of them – not because of the sleeping that occurs there but because of the vandalism, defecation, streetfighting, discarding of contaminated blankets and uneaten food, blocking of walkways, harassment of passersby, and open drug use. NBC News reported that in Los Angeles gang members "hid[e] in plain sight" in Skid Row's tents to "prey on many who live here looking for services and help." In Seattle, police seized crack, heroin, meth, pills, guns, machetes, a sword, purses, tablets, cellphones, watches, and perfume – all from a crime ring run out of tents. In San Jose's now-dismantled "Jungle" encampment, where as many as 300 lived amid the trees, a resident described a lawless zone in the middle of Silicon Valley where murders went uninvestigated.[33]

Encampments imperil the environment, too. In Orange County, workers cleaned thousands of pounds of human waste, and nearly 14,000 hypodermic needles, from Santa Ana River encampments. According to a geologist affiliated with a California water quality control district, "It's a health issue. You know there's E.coli, there's fecalborn coliform in this water from these buckets and their toilets that are all along the stream." Another water district official explained to NBC News: "It's a threat to all the communities around the Bay. All the water flows through the creeks, ends up in the Bay and carries whatever trash, debris and contaminants."[34]

Anti-camping enforcement is also necessary to control risk of wildfire or urban fires. For instance, the Skirball fire that burned more than 400 acres in Los Angeles in 2017 started as a cooking fire at a homeless encampment. Some cities have had to clear encampments abutting grasslands as a precaution. L.A. firefighters now extinguish almost seven fires a day started at encampments or tents, a 211 percent increase from 2018. Some blazes begin when homeless individuals tap into power lines to provide electricity in their tents; others when stoves and barbecues are used in flammable tents.[35]

> *Of course more housing is needed. Of course more mental health services are necessary. But cities have urgent, ongoing, and unignorable health and safety needs to address.*

Many fed-up Californians who live near encampments suffer the daily consequences. Bob Smiland, CEO of Inner-City Arts, a school in Skid Row, was forced by encampments to redirect thousands of dollars into security; his students and teachers jaywalk to avoid the tents that clog the sidewalks.[36] Nearby, a man named Mark Mozgo purchased a small event property only to learn that proliferating tents were driving away the customers he hoped to lure for weddings. He receives text messages like: "I'm sorry, I really like your place, but the street is unacceptable."[37]

Federal court cases decided in 2019, after the *Martin v. City of Boise* decision, show that trial courts mostly allow the closure of encampments, so long as there is a health and safety purpose. In *Butcher v. City of Marysville*, the court found that Marysville lawfully removed some 300–500 members of homeless encampments on the Yuba and Feather Rivers (some residents claiming to have been there for a decade) in order to clear them from flood zones.[38] Or in *Quintero v. City of Santa Cruz*, Santa Cruz closed a 200-person encampment – one plagued by murders and sexual assaults; before doing so, however, the city undertook to talk to 112 individuals there and distribute vouchers for temporary housing and transportation, even if only 30 took the city up on them.[39]

Las Vegas's post-*Martin* ordinance against encampments has intelligent features that make it enforceable and fair. First, the camping prohibition only applies to residential areas and certain downtown commercial areas, in order to limit the scope of the ordinance as to location (though not as to time or manner). Second, enforcement can only occur when shelter is available; the city informs police when beds fill up and at that point enforcement is suspended. Third, the ordinance avoids being punitive. The city declares enforcement a "last resort" and requires officers to notify individuals that their conduct is prohibited before ticketing, as well as to direct them to a shelter or public location where the individuals *can* sleep.[40]

Some cities, forced by the *Martin* decision to allow camping somewhere in the city but lacking sufficient indoor shelters, have designated areas in which camping is allowed. This can be simply a set-aside area or a secured location where the city provides lighting, water, and toilets. Seattle authorizes "transitional encampments" (i.e., encampments for living before a transition to more permanent housing) that are set up by permits, run by "operators," and regulated by mini-codes covering everything from physical size to service requirements.[41] What these approaches all have in common is that they constitute city-approved encampments, a once unthinkable proposition to many city leaders.

Oakland, under incredible pressure from residents to do *something*, has been perhaps the boldest in experimenting with "sanctioned" encampments, where individuals can pitch tents without police interference. Oakland mayor Libby Schaaf called these encampments temporary compromises, born of necessity, but she later soured on them. She told CBS News: "All have ended in fires, unhealthy conditions for residents, let alone the surrounding community. From my experience we have tried it and it has failed." CBS reported that residents were "shocked" when an encampment arose, by city permission, next to a soccer field. "This is . . . where kids play and you are exposing them to hazards and dangers and rodents and needles," one father said. Some of the encampment's homeless residents actually agreed.[42]

Cities also have established parking zones for those living in vehicles. If nothing else, it allows a city to control where such zones arise – for instance, away from business districts or residential areas. This also lets a city better connect individuals with services. And it keeps people from living on the streets themselves, which poses problems that vehicle living does not. San Diego opened three such lots before April 2019; one can accommodate 80 RVs or 200 standard cars.[43]

A Word on the "Criminalization of the Homeless"

A San Francisco police sergeant in 2018 said that his department "realized many years ago that we cannot arrest our way out of the homeless crisis."[44] True. But quality-of-life laws are not designed to get us "out" of the crisis; they are designed to keep streets tolerable while cities attempt longer-term solutions – none of which, alone, will result in any permanent resolution.[45] Consider Bibbo Saab, the owner of a hair salon near San Francisco's Union Square, who gained local fame when he posted videos of a homeless woman undressing herself near the salon's front door. As CBS reported, "He said multiple clients refused to enter his salon because the woman was defecating in front of it. Bibbo called police but, 'they always say the same phrase, "there's nothing we can do."'"[46] That depends on what "do" means: the police can't solve the problem that ails that unfortunate woman. But they can solve the problem facing Saab, by removing the woman.[47]

Quality of life laws in most metropolitan areas should not be framed to castigate or discomfit the homeless. They should be designed to ensure that teachers can take students on field trips without encountering needles that attract little hands; to ensure that store owners do not face slow strangulation by having customers deterred by menacing behavior; that tourists do not fly home disgusted at the sight of individuals staggering around in hospital gowns; that libraries remain places of learning, not places to wash your body.[48]

There is scant demagoguery on the issue. The politicians who pass laws, or the police chiefs and sheriffs who enforce them, rarely find that beating up on the homeless is a political winner.[49] No one on the city councils of Los Angeles, Seattle, Portland, or San Francisco talks of "getting tough" on the homeless or "sending a message" to them. Rather, official action is mostly reactive, responding to the pleas of exasperated residents or merchants, tourism bureaus, or developers. The *New Yorker*'s Nathan Heller, reporting on homelessness in San Francisco, wrote of a supervisor who acted under pressure from constituents: "'I was getting complaints from people who felt horrible complaining.... People who said, "I volunteer in homeless shelters, but I'm at my wit's end."'"[50]

Virtually no one today insists, like the charities of the eighteenth, nineteenth, and early twentieth centuries, that the availability of services should turn on a searching examination of the extent to which a suppliant's own bad choices led to his unfortunate condition. Most of us recognize, instead, that the most important thing to know about a homeless person is that they are a *person*. Most Californians want to help the homeless find roofs, nutrition, counseling, work, safety, stability, warmth, family, and health.[51] Hundreds of local governments together dedicate hundreds of millions of dollars to shelters and services.[52] But cities set themselves up for failure and disappointment (and possibly cycles of punitive, get-tough policy) in self-congratulatory proposals to "solve" the homelessness crisis. It cannot be "solved" any more than poverty or substance abuse or any other tragic aspect of the human condition can be solved. Homelessness can only be *managed*.

It is a human problem, which is why, in the end, the most decisive argument against the use of a heavy hand in controlling homelessness is that it isn't stigma and coercion but compassion and collaboration that, empirically, work best. Here are formerly homeless men and women, who deserve the last word, recounting what helped them escape the streets:

> My boyfriend was homeless for a period of his life because of an abusive parent. . . . [T]he best and most truly invaluable thing he does for the homeless people he meets is he stops and has a real conversation with them. He listens and shares stories and treats them with respect and dignity. He always tells me that it's not the money people need, it's normalcy. . . . Brushing your teeth, combing your hair, saying hello to your neighbor, and spending your day doing normal things and feeling normal. Too many cannot find this normalcy and so they turn to drugs and alcohol to escape their reality. Because they think they'll never feel normal again.

* * *

It's hard to get out of homelessness because each piece a person is missing (a place to live, an income, etc.) makes obtaining all the rest more difficult. Individual contributions can be helpful, but none of them are the solution. People don't panhandle for change to put a down payment on an apartment. Offering food or socks is appreciated, and certainly a good thing to do. But if you want to help people get out of the situation, only charities or public programs are equipped to provide the holistic support people need.

* * *

I remember getting help with free food like day-old bread and free fruit/sandwiches etc., as well as free clothes and I was grateful for all of it. What I remember most though are the people who saw past the mental illness, past the skittish, scared girl and into the human being underneath. The hotel clerk who let me charge my phone and gave me free coffee, no strings attached; the police officer who told me about shelters instead of writing me a ticket; and the shelter worker who chatted with me about some silly show on tv. I always remember those people and when I now work with homeless and disadvantaged people I always look for their humanity even when it is hard to find.[53]

12 COMPASSIONATE ENFORCEMENT

Balancing Public Services and Public Order

Christopher F. Rufo

Fifteen years ago, West Coast cities projected supreme confidence in their ability to solve homelessness. In coordination with the state and federal governments, cities throughout the region established high-profile commissions and released 10-year plans to end homelessness. Then Seattle mayor Greg Nickels declared that homelessness would become a "rare, brief, and one-time" event; James Hahn, who was mayor of Los Angeles, announced the city would create a plan to "move people off the street and into places they can call their own"; current governor and then San Francisco mayor Gavin Newsom promised "not to manage but to end homelessness," praising the city's plan as "brilliant in its simplicity."[1]

Armed with the latest academic studies on the success of Housing First, a program designed to directly provide long-term apartments to the homeless, experts argued that cities could simultaneously end homelessness and save taxpayers money – the Holy Grail of public policy. Philip Mangano, executive director of the US Interagency Council on Homelessness, summarized the prevailing mood: "Five years ago the notion of cities having 10-year plans to end homelessness was naïve and risky. No one thought it was possible. But the new research and new technologies have created such movement and innovation on this issue that it may now be naïve and risky not to have such a plan."[2]

These ambitions turned out to be delusions. Hahn's plan to end homelessness in Los Angeles collapsed before it even began; Newsom watched homelessness expand in San Francisco and then expand statewide; in Seattle, Nickels has been immortalized in a series of tent cities called "Nickelsvilles."[3] In nearly every major West Coast city, homelessness is worse than ever before – tents line the sidewalks and some downtown neighborhoods have turned into

Latin American–style *favelas*, with open-air drug markets and booming black-market economies.[4]

The new conventional wisdom is dominated by pessimism – homelessness is intractable, a permanent feature of the urban landscape. Political leaders have abandoned any pretension of "abolishing homelessness," focusing instead on strategies of containment and "harm reduction." But this, too, is wrong. Homelessness is neither intractable nor permanent, and policies of "harm reduction" have shown little capacity to reduce homelessness. Rather than continue down this path, West Coast political leaders should learn from other cities, including Houston, that have pioneered another model – compassionate enforcement – that has demonstrated remarkable success over the past decade. Although West Coast cities have dominated the headlines with bad news, cities such as Houston, which has reduced homelessness by 54 percent since 2011, show that another way is possible.

First, we must break down a series of misconceptions that have prevented major cities from successfully reducing homelessness. The conventional wisdom holds that "homelessness is a national problem," and many service providers, local officials, and state governors have insisted that the federal government is responsible. This serves a dual purpose: it shifts the blame to the national executive and obscures the failure of the political class in West Coast cities. But this oft-repeated nugget of conventional wisdom is patently false. The facts: between 2009 and 2019, homelessness decreased 10 percent nationwide; moreover, on a geographic basis, homelessness declined in 39 states.[5] The reality is that homelessness is not distributed evenly across the country. It has become more concentrated in a handful of states, particularly California, Oregon, and Washington, which now account for one-third of the total homeless population nationwide.[6]

The next step in the current debate is to answer the question "why?" One of the most common arguments from activists and political leaders is that homelessness is concentrated in certain cities and states because of weather. First, although it is obviously easier to live on the streets in Los Angeles than in Chicago during a long winter, weather alone does not explain the distribution of homelessness in the United States. As the Council of Economic Advisers (CEA) has shown, the rate of homelessness is high in California cities but low in

Florida cities, which also have warm winter climates.[7] Overall, according to the CEA analysis, unsheltered homelessness is two to four times higher than predicted according to weather in California, Washington, and Oregon, and lower than predicted according to weather in Florida, Arizona, Tennessee, Louisiana, and Mississippi.

We believe there is a better explanation for the current distribution of homelessness in the United States: public policy. Despite suffering from high rates of addiction and mental illness, the homeless are fundamentally rational actors; they respond to economic, policy, and cultural incentives in their own world. For the most part, researchers have analyzed homelessness according to middle-class norms, believing that the homeless respond primarily to measures of poverty, rental prices, and housing policy. But it's important to make this distinction: the homeless have a different set of incentives than the average citizen; their world is not like the world of the middle class.

In order to formulate successful policies, it's essential to understand the domain of unsheltered homelessness. The facts, which have become taboo in progressive cities, are simple: 75 percent of the unsheltered homeless have a serious addiction, 78 percent have a mental illness, and, as a group, they are nearly 100 times more likely to commit crimes and get booked into jail than the average citizen.[8] It's a world of tangled pathologies, driven by the economics of the drug trade, the psychology of addiction, and the culture of transient encampments. Although this presents a complex challenge, it doesn't mean that the unsheltered homeless are "irrational." In fact, just the opposite is true – as a population, the homeless are highly responsive to public policy, which has shaped migration and population patterns to an extent that has not been appreciated in the popular discourse.

In nearly every major West Coast city, homelessness is worse than ever before – tents line the sidewalks and some downtown neighborhoods have turned into Latin American-style favelas, with open-air drug markets and booming black-market economies.

One can begin with a simple story that illustrates the larger point. The Venice Boulevard underpass on the border of Los Angeles and Culver City is one of thousands of concrete structures in Los Angeles County, but there's a curious detail: The Los Angeles side is full of tents and the Culver City side is empty.[9] Why? As neighboring cities, Los Angeles and Culver City have the same regional economy, climate, and rental prices –

in fact, Culver City is slightly more expensive than Los Angeles.[10] The difference is public policy. Los Angeles has effectively decriminalized public camping and drug consumption; Culver City enforces the law. After two Los Angeles city councilmen complained in the *Los Angeles Times* that Culver City was pushing its homeless into Los Angeles, Culver City mayor Jeffrey Cooper shot back in a letter to the editor: "The encampment under the 405 Freeway on Venice Boulevard...has been the scene of numerous violent crimes. The Los Angeles Police Department does not check in with the homeless people living there nearly as often as Culver City police do. If I was a homeless person inclined to do drugs and commit crimes, I would feel safer in Los Angeles than Culver City, whose police are there to protect all residents."[11]

The principle in the Venice Boulevard experiment provides a useful framework for reexamining the geography of homelessness. In California, the data is consistent with the enforcement principle: across the state, the homeless migrate toward the most permissive policy environments. In Los Angeles County, 35 percent of the homeless migrated to the county after becoming homeless elsewhere, including 19 percent who traveled from another state.[12] In San Francisco County, 30 percent of the homeless migrated there after becoming homeless in another location; an additional 6 percent became homeless after living in San Francisco for less than a year.[13] The *San Francisco Chronicle* estimates that 450 chronically homeless individuals migrate to the city each year because of the "perception that it is a sanctuary for people who are unwilling to participate in programs designed to get them off, and keep them off, a life in the streets."[14]

The numbers from the Seattle metropolitan area further bolster the enforcement hypothesis. According to city data, an astonishing 51 percent of the homeless migrated there after becoming homeless somewhere else.[15] In the middle-class logic of the conventional wisdom, this would be an irrational choice – an individual with no shelter or stable source of income would not move to one of the most expensive cities in the country. But the homeless operate under a different set of assumptions and incentives. In their world, it is a rational choice – they are strongly incentivized to move to the most permissive environment. In a research survey of homeless migrants in Seattle, 15 percent said they came to access homeless services, 10 percent came for legal marijuana, and 16 percent were transients who were "traveling or visiting" when they decided to set up camp.[16] But this may dramatically understate the largest incentive of all: the de facto legalization of street camping, drug consumption, and property crime. As former Seattle public safety advisor Scott Lindsay has shown, the city is now home to a large population of homeless "prolific offenders" who commit property crimes to feed their addictions – and are rarely held to account by the criminal justice system.[17]

Some will deride these conclusions as an endorsement of an "enforcement-only" approach that "criminalizes homelessness" – but they'd be wrong. The lesson is not that cities should withhold help from the homeless; it's that cities must balance the provision of public services with the maintenance of public order. Cities that fail to acknowledge the relationship between permissiveness, migration, and rates of homelessness will fail to make progress.

Houston is the American city that has best demonstrated the power of "compassionate enforcement." Harris County is a moderate district, with conservative suburban areas and a liberal urban core. Houston mayor Sylvester Turner is a Democrat, but his rhetoric on homelessness is a world apart from the language of Los Angeles, San Francisco, and Seattle.

"It is simply not acceptable for people to live on the streets; it is not good for them, and it is not good for the city," Turner has said. "We will tackle this complicated issue, and we will do it humanely with a meaningful approach that balances the needs of the homeless and the concerns of neighborhoods they impact."[18]

Houston's policy is a perfect example of what Turner calls a "tough love" approach. The city has built permanent supportive housing for the chronically homeless, built a coalition of nonprofit partners, and lobbied the state government for more mental health and addiction services. At the same time, Turner has enforced a strict ban on public camping and proposed a citywide campaign to discourage citizens from giving money to panhandlers. The Harris County Sheriff's Homeless Outreach Team attempts to connect the homeless with services but also enforces the law. The sheriff's office plainly acknowledges that "mental illness and substance abuse are common in [the homeless] population" and recognizes that it must maintain order in residential neighborhoods. The team shuts down tent cities and conducts regular cleanups, discouraging the kind of permanent encampment culture seen in West Coast cities.

The results have been stunning. Over the past eight years, Houston has reduced its homeless population by 54 percent.[19] These outcomes lay waste to the conventional wisdom. Houston has warmer winters than Seattle, Portland, Sacramento, and San Jose.[20] Clearly, the weather cannot explain the outcomes in Houston, which defy the logic of progressive politicians and social scientists with a "data-driven" explanation of homelessness.

Some analysts have suggested that Houston's approach worked because the city built permanent supportive housing, created a coalition of partners, and implemented advanced data tracking.[21] But every major West Coast city has followed a similar approach. Seattle, San Francisco, and Los Angeles have spent billions on permanent supportive housing and subsidized apartments, hosted conferences and working groups to increase coordination, and implemented the same Homeless Management Information System data tracking as Houston. And yet, since 2011, homelessness has increased 15 percent in Los Angeles, 24 percent in San Francisco, and 25 percent in Seattle. If these interventions worked in Houston, why didn't they work in Los Angeles, San Francisco, and Seattle?

The truth is hiding in plain sight. Houston achieved different results because it had different policies. It is correct that, like many West Coast cities, Houston built permanent supportive housing for the chronically homeless and increased services across the board. But unlike Los Angeles, San Francisco, and Seattle, Houston avoided the policies that enable and incentivize the worst aspects of street homelessness. Where a Seattle politician opposes hosing down feces-covered sidewalks because hoses have racist connotations, Houston fights in the courts for the right to clean up encampments.[22] Where California leaders push for supervised injection sites and decriminalizing thefts under $950, Houston pushes for tighter restrictions on aggressive panhandling, window washing, and other "street obstructions."[23]

What prevents West Coast cities from implementing the same policies as Houston? Political culture. According to social scientist Jonathan Haidt, liberals and conservatives operate on very different moral foundations.[24] Liberals base their views primarily on the values of care and fairness – that is, they value compassion above all other concerns. Conservatives, on the other hand, "construct moral systems more evenly upon five psychological foundations," showing concern for care and fairness, but also valuing authority, purity, and in-group loyalty.

Haidt's theory provides a useful framework for understanding why progressive cities have been unable to reduce homelessness, despite billions in public spending. Progressives, according to Haidt, have an "unconstrained vision" of the world and "an optimistic view of human nature and human perfectibility." On homelessness, the basic progressive view is that the homeless are victims of circumstance and inequality and simply need a helping hand to improve their lives.

However, this view has three moral blind spots.

Houston's policy is a perfect example of what Turner calls a "tough love" approach. The city has built permanent supportive housing for the chronically homeless, built a coalition of nonprofit partners, and lobbied the state government for more mental health and addiction services. At the same time, Turner has enforced a strict ban on public camping and proposed a citywide campaign to discourage citizens from giving money to panhandlers.

First, because progressives discount the moral foundation of authority, they dismiss concerns about crime, disorder, and violence and generally don't see the need for law enforcement the same way conservatives do. In fact, West Coast progressives have sought to decriminalize public camping, drug consumption, and property crimes – they view authority as the problem, not part of the solution.

Second, because progressives are less interested in the moral foundation of purity, they overlook and excuse the filth associated with street camping. Homeless encampments have proven to be havens for trash, needles, drugs, human waste, and infectious diseases, and yet, West Coast progressives have fought to "stop the sweeps" of tent cities and filed lawsuits against encampment cleanups. They prioritize "care for our curbside neighbors" over sanitation, cleanliness, and public health concerns.

Third, because progressives discount the moral foundation of in-group loyalty, they do not see significant homeless in-migration as a problem. They make no distinction between the local and nonlocal homeless populations, and they reject concerns about cities creating a magnet effect as "xenophobic" and "homeless-hating." Put simply, in progressive cities, it's all compassion and no enforcement, which creates an unintended cycle of permissiveness, enablement, and disorder.

Critics might argue that this is an unfair assessment of the views of homeless service providers in West Coast cities. They might point to outreach teams as examples of authority, to sanitation plans as examples of purity, and to bus programs as examples of in-group loyalty. However, at the practical level, the homeless-services apparatus has become one of the most ideologically extreme sectors of West Coast government. In Seattle, the regional homelessness authority recently held its annual conference on the theme of "Decolonizing Our Collective Work," with sessions designed to "[interrogate] the current structures of power" and "examine the legacies of structural racism in our systems, and co-design a path towards liberation with black, indigenous, brown and other marginalized communities."[25]

As part of the conference, the agency hired transgender stripper Beyoncé Black St. James to perform a drag show, give lap dances, and kiss attendees. What does any of this have to do with reducing homelessness? Nothing. It's about repeating the nostrums of social justice, radicalizing homeless-services providers, and advancing the larger progressive political project. It's not hard to understand why these agencies have been unable to reduce homelessness – any entity that prioritizes "decolonizing our collective work" over practical solutions to homelessness is doomed to fail.

What does the future hold for American cities and homelessness? Sadly, more of the same. Policies can change quickly, but ideologies have much deeper roots. In the near term, there will likely be a continued redistribution of the homelessness crisis toward the warmest, most expensive, and most permissive cities, focused primarily in the coastal enclaves of California, Oregon, and Washington. West Coast cities have recently announced unprecedented multibillion-dollar expenditures on homelessness, but money alone cannot overcome the deficiencies of their political cultures. If the progressive political class continues to discount the moral values of authority, purity, and loyalty, it will find itself unable to cope with the dark side of homelessness: addiction, crime, violence, squalor, and disease. If the homeless-services apparatus continues to prioritize political convictions over practical plans, it will waste billions on narrow ideological programs that fail to address the need for both compassion and enforcement.

Meanwhile, this presents an opportunity for cities willing to try a different approach. As Houston has demonstrated, local leaders can meaningfully reduce homelessness through a strategy of "tough love" – leading with the provision of shelter and services but maintaining the public order through outreach, cleanups, and enforcement of anti-camping laws. Some progressive leaders have recently complained that enforcement policies shift the burden of homelessness onto the largest cities. But this is a baseless argument. Cities compete on taxes, infrastructure, amenities, and a thousand other policy choices – the presence of unsheltered homelessness is just as legitimate as any of them. Small and medium-sized cities should not lower their standards of public order; rather, it is incumbent upon their neighboring cities to adopt a similar approach and reduce the "magnet effect" of their own permissive policies.

In the long term, the best possible outcome is for all cities to band together and adopt a similar approach of compassionate enforcement. The homeless are, like anyone, responsive to public policies in their domain. If cities can close down negative pathways – public encampments, open drug consumption, and uncontrolled property crimes – they will be able to redirect the homeless toward better outcomes. In cities such as Los Angeles, San Francisco, and Seattle, political leaders must fundamentally reorient their policies across the full spectrum of psychological foundations, balancing care and fairness with authority, purity, and loyalty. They must acknowledge the limitations of their own worldview and think more broadly about the moral dimension of homelessness.

There are more than 180,000 people on the streets of West Coast cities, dependent on the choices of policymakers in the coming years. Ultimately, compassion must be measured not by good intentions but by outcomes. If progressive political leaders want to live up to their own values, they must demonstrate results.

ACKNOWLEDGMENTS

A special thanks to Sally Pipes, PRI president and CEO. We would also like to thank Tim Anaya and Rowena Itchon for their tireless efforts, support, and guidance. Their advice and input has vastly improved this book, and their counsel is simply invaluable.

CONTRIBUTORS

KERRY JACKSON is an independent journalist and opinion writer with extensive experience covering politics and public policy. Currently a fellow with the Center for California Reform at the Pacific Research Institute (PRI), Kerry writes weekly op-eds and blog posts on statewide issues and occasional books and policy papers.

He is the author of *Living in Fear in California*, a book that explores well-meaning changes to California's public safety laws enacted in recent years that have undermined safe communities and offers reforms that strike a balance between the state's obligation to crime victims and the rights of the accused and convicted.

In 2017, he wrote *Unaffordable: How Government Made California's Housing Shortage a Crisis and How Free Market Ideas Can Restore Affordability and Supply*, an issue brief on California's housing crisis, which won bipartisan praise. His 2018 brief on poverty in California, *Good Intentions: How California's Anti-Poverty Programs Aren't Delivering and How the Private Sector Can Lift More People Out of Poverty*, garnered national attention for his *Los Angeles Times* op-ed asking, "Why is liberal California the poverty capital of America?"

Jackson is a leading commentator on California's growing homeless crisis. In 2019, he coauthored (with Dr. Wayne Winegarden) a brief on San Francisco's homeless crisis, which was presented to Mayor London Breed's administration. His commentaries have been published in the *Los Angeles Times*, *San Francisco Chronicle*, CalMatters, *City Journal*, *Daily Caller*, *New York Observer*, *Orange County Register*, *Bakersfield Californian*, *San Francisco Examiner*, *Fresno Bee*, *Ventura County Star*, *Forbes*, and *Fox and Hounds Daily*, among others. He regularly appears on radio and television programs commenting on the problems affecting California. Jackson has been a past guest on National Public Radio, One America News Network, Newsmax TV, and *The Dr. Drew Show*, among others.

Before coming to PRI, Jackson spent 18 years writing editorials on domestic and foreign policy for Investor's Business Daily (IBD) and three years as the assistant director of public affairs for the American Legislative Exchange Council. He has written for the American

Media Institute and Real Clear Investigations and edited "The Growth Manifesto" for the Committee to Unleash Prosperity.

CHRISTOPHER F. RUFO is an adjunct fellow at PRI. He is a filmmaker, writer, and policy researcher. He has directed four films for PBS, Netflix, and international television, including his latest film, *America Lost*, which tells the story of three "forgotten American cities." He is the director of the Discovery Institute's Center on Wealth and Poverty and a contributing editor at *City Journal*, where he covers poverty, homelessness, addiction, crime, and other afflictions. Christopher graduated magna cum laude from Georgetown University, was a Claremont Institute Lincoln fellow, and has appeared on NPR, CNN, ABC, CBS, HLN, and Fox News.

JOSEPH TARTAKOVSKY is the former deputy solicitor general of Nevada, an attorney specializing in constitutional and appellate law in California, and the author of *The Lives of the Constitution: Ten Exceptional Minds that Shaped America's Supreme Law*. He is also a Pacific Research Institute fellow in legal studies. His writing has appeared in the *New York Times*, *Wall Street Journal*, and *Los Angeles Times*, among other publications.

WAYNE WINEGARDEN, PhD, is a senior fellow in business and economics, Pacific Research Institute, as well as the director of PRI's Center for Medical Economics and Innovation. Dr. Winegarden's policy research explores the connection between macroeconomic policies and economic outcomes, with a focus on fiscal policy, the health care industry, and the energy sector.

As director of the Center for Medical Economics and Innovation, Dr. Winegarden spearheads research and advances policies that support the continued viability and vitality of the US biomedical and pharmaceutical industries to the benefit of patients and overall economic growth.

Dr. Winegarden's columns have been published in the *Wall Street Journal*, *Chicago Tribune*, *Investor's Business Daily*, Forbes.com, and *USA Today*. He was previously economics faculty at Marymount University, has testified before the US Congress, has been interviewed and quoted in such media as CNN and Bloomberg Radio, and is asked to present his research findings at policy conferences and meetings.

Dr. Winegarden is also the principal of an economic advisory firm that advises clients on the economic, business, and investment implications from changes in broader macroeconomic trends and government policies. Clients have included Fortune 500 companies, financial organizations, small businesses, and trade associations. Previously, Dr. Winegarden worked as a business economist in Hong Kong and New York City and as a policy economist for policy and trade associations in Washington, D.C. Dr. Winegarden received his BA, MA, and PhD in economics from George Mason University.

STEPHEN MOORE is co-founder of the Committee to Unleash Prosperity. He served as senior economic advisor to Donald Trump during the 2016 presidential campaign. He is the former economic editor at the *Wall Street Journal* editorial board.

APPENDIX

Data Snapshot
California's Growing Homeless Problem Over the Years by City

San Francisco

San Francisco Biennial Point-in-Time Count

2005	6,248
2007	6,377
2009	6,514
2011	6,455
2013	6,436
2015	6,686
2017	6,986
2019	8,035

Source: San Francisco Human Services Agency

Los Angeles

Los Angeles City Homeless Population, By Year

2013	22,393
2015	25,686
2016	28,464
2017	34,189
2018	31,285
2019	36,300
2020	41,290

Los Angeles County (All Cities) Homeless Population, By Year

2013	40,149
2014	39,000+
2015	44,359
2016	46,874
2017	57,794
2018	52,765
2019	58,936
2020	66,436

Source: Los Angeles Homeless Services Authority

San Diego

San Diego City and County Point-in-Time Homeless Count

2011	9,020
2012	9,638
2013	8,879
2014	8,506
2015	8,742
2016	8,692
2017	9,116
2018	8,125
2019	8,102
2020	8,102

Source: Regional Task Force on the Homeless, Annual Point-in-Time Count

San Jose

San Jose Biennial Point-in-Time Count

2007	4,309
2009	4,193
2011	4,034
2013	4,770
2015	4,063
2017	4,350
2019	6,097

Source: City of San Jose, Homeless Census & Survey, Comprehensive Report, 2019

Sacramento

Sacramento County Point-in-Time Count

2013	2,538
2015	2,659
2017	3,665
2019	5,570

Source: Sacramento Steps Forward

NOTES

CHAPTER 1

1 "The 2019 Annual Homeless Report (AHAR) to Congress," Part 1: Point-in-Time Estimates of Homelessness, US Department of Housing and Urban Development, Office of Community Planning and Development, January 2020, p. 13.

2 "The 2017 Annual Homeless Report (AHAR) to Congress," Part 1: Point-in-Time Estimates of Homelessness, US Department of Housing and Urban Development, Office of Community Planning and Development, December 2017, p. 13.

3 "The 2019 Annual Homeless Report," Part 1, p. 12.

4 "The 2019 Annual Homeless Report," Part 1, pp. 10, 12.

5 "The 2019 Annual Homeless Report," Part 1, pp. 66, 68.

6 "The 2019 Annual Homeless Report," Part 1, p. 69.

7 Jill Cowan, "San Francisco's Homeless Population Is Much Bigger Than Thought, City Data Suggests," *New York Times*, November 19, 2019.

8 Cowan, "San Francisco's Homeless Population."

9 Kerry Jackson, "Will Newsom's Second Chance at Reducing Homelessness Succeed?," *Right by the Bay*, Pacific Research Institute, August 1, 2018.

10 2020 Greater Los Angeles Homeless Count Results, Los Angeles Homeless Services Authority, July 6, 2020.

11 Benjamin Oreskes, "L.A. County Is Counting Homeless People This Week. Here's Everything You Need to Know," *Los Angeles Times*, January 21, 2020.

12 Gale Holland, "L.A.'s Homeless Surged 75 Percent in Six Years. Here's Why the Crisis Has Been Decades in the Making," *Los Angeles Times*, February 1, 2018.

13 "Homelessness on City of San Diego Streets Drops by 12 percent in Annual Count," Office of Mayor Kevin L. Faulconer, April 28, 2020.

14 "Homelessness Drops in San Diego," City News Service, KPBS, April 29, 2020.

15 City of San Jose, Homeless Census & Survey, Comprehensive Report, 2019.

16 Emily Deruy, "San Jose: 42 percent Spike in Homeless Population," *Mercury News*, May 17, 2019.

17 Cynthia Hubert, "In Midtown, a Daily Fight for Cleanliness and Safety as Homelessness Surges," *Sacramento Bee*, October 17, 2017.

18 Tim Anaya, "On Homelessness, Sacramento Is Becoming More Like San Francisco . . . and That's Not a Good Thing," *Right By the Bay*, Pacific Research Institute, October 30, 2017.

19 Kevin Fagan, "California's Homelessness Crisis Expands to Country," *San Francisco Chronicle*, September 13, 2017.

Notes

20   Tonya Mosley and Cristina Kim, "'We Are Better Than This': California Gov. Gavin Newsom on His New Plan to Address Homelessness," *Here and Now*, National Public Radio and WBUR Boston, January 16, 2020.

21   Chris Nichols, "PolitiFact California: Did California's Homeless Population Decrease Since 2005? That's What Gov. Gavin Newsom Said This Week," Capital Public Radio, February 20, 2020.

22   "85 percent of Homeless People Have Chronic Health Conditions," *Science Daily*, August 24, 2011.

23   Samantha Raphelson, "San Francisco Squalor: City Streets Strewn with Trash, Needles and Human Feces," National Public Radio, August 1, 2018.

24   Dan Simon, "The Impact Homelessness and the Opioid Crisis Are Having on San Francisco Streets," CNN, December 28, 2018.

25   Bigad Shaban, Robert Campos, Tony Rutanooshedech, and Michael Horn, "Diseased Streets," NBC Bay Area, February 18, 2018, updated December 6, 2018.

26   Shaban, Campos, Rutanooshedech, and Horn, "Diseased Streets."

27   Simon, "The Impact Homelessness and the Opioid Crisis Are Having."

28   Raphelson, "San Francisco Squalor."

29   Phillip Matier and Andrew Ross, "SF's Appalling Street Life Repels Residents – Now It's Driven Away a Convention," *SF Gate*, July 2, 2018.

30   Ari Levy, "Oracle Will Move Its Annual OpenWorld Conference to Las Vegas Because San Francisco Is Too Expensive," CNBC, December 10, 2019.

31   Phil Matier, "Little Bang for the Buck: SF's Spending on Street Cleaning Not Really Doing Much," San Francisco Chronicle, December 22, 2019.

32   Dianne de Guzman, "BART's Weekend, Night Ridership Drop by 10 Million," *SF Gate*, February 12, 2020.

CHAPTER 2

1   Gale Holland, "L.A. Spent $619 Million on Homelessness Last Year. Has It Made a Difference?," *Los Angeles Times*, May 11, 2019, https://www.latimes.com/local/california/la-me-ln-homeless-housing-count-20190511-story.html.

2   "Proposed Budget: Mayor London N. Breed," Mayor's Office of Public Policy and Finance, June 2019, https://sfmayor.org/sites/default/files/CSF_Budget_Book_June_2019_Final_Web_REV2.pdf; Adam Brinklow, "SF Had a Renaissance in Homeless Aid This Decade – and It Barely Mattered," *San Francisco Curbed*, December 19, 2019, https://sf.curbed.com/2019/12/19/21027974/san-francisco-homeless-decade-2010s-kositsky-navigation-center-friedenbach.

3   For more information on Rapid Re-Housing, see Corporation for Supportive Housing, "Homelessness Prevention & Rapid Re-Housing Program California," https://www.cibhs.org/sites/main/files/file-attachments/homelesspreventionfundsabbreviated.pdf; and Orange County United Way, "Housing," https://www.unitedwayoc.org/how-we-are-doing-more/housing/rapid-re-housing.

4   For more information on Project Homekey see "Governor Newsom Visits

Project Roomkey Site in Bay Area to Announce 'Homekey,' the Next Phase in State's COVID-19 Response to Protect Homeless Californians," Office of Governor Gavin Newsom, June 30, 2020, https://www.gov.ca.gov/2020/06/30/governor-newsom-visits-project-roomkey-site-in-bay-area-to-announce-homekey-the-next-phase-in-states-covid-19-response-to-protect-homeless-californians.

5   "Homelessness in California," California State Auditor, Report Number: 2017-112, https://www.auditor.ca.gov/reports/2017-112/chapters.html.

6   Daniel Flaming, Halil Toros, and Patrick Burns, "Home Not Found: The Cost of Homelessness in Silicon Valley," *Economic Roundtable* (2015), https://www.sccgov.org/sites/osh/ContinuumofCare/ReportsandPublications/Documents/Santa%20Clara%20County%20CostStudyReport.pdf.

7   Flaming, Toros, and Burns, "Home Not Found."

8   Flaming, Toros, and Burns, "Home Not Found."

9   "Homelessness and Health Care," California Health Care Foundation, https://www.chcf.org/topic/homelessness-health-care.

10 "Homelessness in California."

11 Anna Gorman, "Medieval Diseases Are Infecting California's Homeless," *Atlantic*, March 8, 2019, https://www.theatlantic.com/health/archive/2019/03/typhus-tuberculosis-medieval-diseases-spreading-homeless/584380.

12 Chris Woodyard, "As Homeless Are Suffering, Risk of Hepatitis, Typhus and Other Diseases Is Growing," *USA Today*, July 10, 2019, https://www.usatoday.com/story/news/nation/2019/06/18/homeless-homelessness-disease-outbreaks-hepatitis-public-health/1437242001.

13 Lyanne Melendez, "Pier 39 Business Owner to San Francisco Leaders: Stop Ignoring Issues of Homelessness, Dirty Streets," ABC News, December 12, 2019, https://abc7news.com/sf-tourism-pier39-pier-39-homelessness/5750312; Christien Kafton, "Worsening Homelessness Hurting Castro District Businesses, Tourism," Fox KTVU, February 26, 2020; https://www.ktvu.com/news/worsening-homelessness-hurting-castro-district-businesses-tourism; David Montanaro, "LA Business Owners Fed Up with Homeless Crisis: Mayor Keeps Promising Action, but 'There Is No Improvement,'" Fox News, July 12, 2019, https://www.foxnews.com/us/los-angeles-business-owners-fed-up-homeless-crisis.

14 Brock Keeling, "Major Medical Group Cancels San Francisco Convention due to Safety Concerns," Curbed San Francisco, July 3, 2018, https://sf.curbed.com/2018/7/3/17531240/convention-moscone-center-homeless-crime.

15 State of California, Department of Finance, E-2, *California County Population Estimates and Components of Change by Year, July 1, 2010–2019*, December 2019, http://www.dof.ca.gov/Forecasting/Demographics/Estimates/E-2 (emphasis added).

16 "SOI Tax Stats – Migration Data – 2017–18," *Internal Revenue Service Statistics of Income*, https://www.irs.gov/statistics/soi-tax-stats-migration-data-2017-2018 (accessed July 31, 2020).

Notes

17 "Bay Area Homelessness: A Regional View of a Regional Crisis," Bay Area Council Economic Institute, April 2019.

18 "Bay Area Homelessness."

19 "Terner Center Research Series: The Cost of Building Housing," Terner Center for Housing Innovation UC Berkeley, https://ternercenter.berkeley.edu/construction-costs-series#:~:text=Affordable%20Housing%20Costs%3A%20 The%20cost,and%20regulation)%20impact%20affordable%20housing.

20 "The Cost of Building Housing."

21 Chris Woodyard, "$700k for an Apartment? The Cost to Solve the Homeless Crisis Is Soaring in Los Angeles," *USA Today*, August 20, 2019, https://www. usatoday.com/story/news/nation/2019/08/20/homeless-people-los-angeles-la-builds-pricey-koreatown-apartments/1984064001.

22 "State of California Debt Affordability Report," California State Treasurer, October 2019; https://www.treasurer.ca.gov/publications/dar/2019.pdf.

23 "Ending Chronic Homelessness Saves Taxpayers Money," National Alliance to End Homelessness, http://endhomelessness.org/wp-content/uploads/ 2017/06/Cost-Savings-from-PSH.pdf.

CHAPTER 3

1 See Kenneth L. Kusmer, *Down & Out, On the Road: The Homeless in American History* (New York: Oxford University Press, 2002), 13–34.

2 *Briant v. Lyons*, 29 La. Ann. 64, 65 (1877); *Bethune v. Wilkins*, 8 Ga. 118, 121 (1850) (financial distress); *Fetterhoff v. Paul*, 73 Ill. 173, 174 (1874); *Edwards v. Morrow*, 12 La. Ann. 887, 887 (1857); *Phelps v. Porter*, 40 Ga. 485, 486–87 (1869) (loss of caretaker); *Mitchell v. Mitchell*, 40 Ga. 11, 12 (1869); *Pinkston v. Pinkston*, 1867 WL 6977, at *1 (Ky. Jan. 13, 1867) (disability).

3 Kusmer, *Down & Out*, vii, 4–12.

4 Gale Holland, "L.A. Spent $619 Million on Homelessness Last Year. Has It Made a Difference?," *Los Angeles Times*, May 11, 2019, https://www.latimes. com/local/california/la-me-ln-homeless-housing-count-20190511-story.html; see also Kevin Fixler, "Rohnert Park to Spend up to $450,000 More on New Homeless Initiatives," *Santa Rosa Press-Democrat*, August 18, 2019, https:// www.pressdemocrat.com/news/9907977-181/rohnert-park-to-spend-up.

5 Kusmer, *Down & Out*, 13.

6 Kusmer, *Down & Out*, 15.

7 Kusmer, *Down & Out*, 37, 43.

8 See, e.g., Kusmer, *Down & Out*, 27.

9 *Cohens v. Virginia*, 19 U.S. 264, 284–85 (1821) (1804 law).

10 *Mayor, Aldermen & Commonalty of City of New York v. Miln*, 36 U.S. 102, 106 (1837).

11 *Miln*, 36 U.S. at 142–43.

12 See *In re Tiburcio Parrott*, 1 F. 481, 494 (C.C.D. Cal. 1880).

13 *Edwards v. California*, 314 U.S. 160, 170–71 (1941).

14 *Edwards*, 1941 WL 52965 (U.S. Supreme Court Brief for California), *8–10, 14.

15   Kusmer, *Down & Out*, 221.

16   *Edwards*, 314 U.S. at 174.

17   *Edwards*, 314 U.S. at 177.

18   *Papachristou v. City of Jacksonville*, 405 U.S. 156, 161 & n.4 (1972).

19   *Edelman v. California*, 344 U.S. 357, 364-65 (1953) (Black, J., dissenting);
     D.C. v. Hunt, 163 F. 2d 833, 835 (D.C. Cir. 1947) ("A vagrant is a probable
     criminal; and the purpose of the statute is to prevent crimes which may
     likely flow from his mode of life.").

20   *Edelman*, 344 U.S. at 358; see also *Winters v. New York*, 333 U.S. 507, 540
     (1948) (Frankfurter, J., dissenting) ("[Laws] that seek to control 'vagrancy'
     ... are in a class by themselves, in view of the familiar abuses to which they
     are put. Definiteness is designedly avoided so as to allow the net to be cast
     at large, to enable men to be caught who are vaguely undesirable in the eyes
     of police and prosecution, although not chargeable with any particular
     offense.").

21   *Edelman*, 344 U.S. at 364-65.

22   *Shuttlesworth v. City of Birmingham*, 382 U.S. 87, 88 (1965).

23   *Shuttlesworth*, 382 U.S. at 101-02 (Fortas, J., concurring).

24   *Papachristou*, 405 U.S. at 158-60.

25   *Papachristou*, 405 U.S. 156, 157 n.1. By this point, such laws had been under
     sustained judicial attack and invalidation by state supreme and other courts.
     See, e.g., *Goldman v. Knecht*, 295 F. Supp. 897, 906 (D. Colo. 1969) ("Selec-
     tion of violators will necessarily be an arbitrary process based on the personal
     views of the arresting officer or the philosophy of the court hearing the
     case."); *Wheeler v. Goodman*, 306 F. Supp. 58, 62 (W.D.N.C. 1969), *vacated*,
     401 U.S. 987 (1971) ("Here plaintiffs' real offense (to the police) consisted of
     their being hippies. They were at home - not wandering about idly or other-
     wise. It was enough to initiate oppressive police action that plaintiffs seemed
     'vaguely undesirable,' just as the Negroes in *Wright* seemed undesirable in a
     'white' park."); *Smith v. Hill*, 285 F. Supp. 556, 560 (E.D.N.C. 1968) ("The
     ordinance sweeps so broadly that it may be invoked, at the whim of the
     authorities, against every member of the community who is not living in the
     style to which the particular authorities set as a standard."); *Fenster v. Leary*,
     20 N.Y. 2d 309, 315-16 (1967) ("It is also obvious that today the only per-
     sons arrested and prosecuted as common-law vagrants are alcoholic dere-
     licts and other unfortunates, whose only crime, if any, is against themselves,
     and whose main offense usually consists in their leaving the environs of skid
     row and disturbing, by their presence the sensibilities of residents of nicer
     parts of the community, or suspected criminals, with respect to whom the
     authorities do not have enough evidence to make a proper arrest or secure a
     conviction on the crime suspected. As to the former, it seems clear that they
     are more properly objects of the welfare laws and public health programs
     than of the criminal law."); *Parker v. Mun. Judge of City of Las Vegas*, 83 Nev.
     214, 216 (1967) ("It simply is not a crime to be unemployed, without funds,

and in a public place. To punish the unfortunate for this circumstance debases society. The comment of Justice Douglas is relevant: 'How can we hold our heads high and still confuse with crime the need for welfare or the need for work?' Douglas, *Vagrancy and Arrest on Suspicion*, 70 Yale L.J. 1, 12 (1960)."); *People v. Belcastro*, 356 Ill. 144, 150 (1934) ("We must hold the amendment of 1933 to the Vagrancy Act to be void, not only because it is arbitrary and unreasonable legislation and will deprive citizens of their liberty without due process of law, in violation of the state and Federal Constitutions, but also because it clothes administrative officers with arbitrary and discriminatory powers"); *Ex parte Hudgins*, 86 W. Va. 526 (1920) ("If a citizen, say of fifty or fifty-five years of age, had worked diligently earlier in life, and had laid up a competency with which to support himself and his dependents in his or their stations of life, that he might for the rest of his days live in comparative ease and freedom from the burdens of his earlier years, he could not defend himself on that account nor escape the penalties imposed for a violation of the statute, characterizing him as a vagrant and punishable as such. Can such a statute find justification in the police power of the state?"); *City of St. Louis v. Gloner*, 210 Mo. 502 (1908) ("The defendant had the unquestioned right to go where he pleased, and to stop and remain upon the corner of any street that he might desire, so long as he conducted himself in a decent and orderly manner, disturbing no one, nor interfering with any one's right to the use of the street.").

26 *Papachristou*, 405 U.S. at 171.
27 *Papachristou*, 405 U.S. at 163.
28 *Papachristou*, 405 U.S. at 162 (citations and quotation marks omitted).
29 *Kolender v. Lawson*, 461 U.S. 352, 353–54 (1983).
30 *Kolender*, 461 U.S. at 360 (quotation marks omitted).

CHAPTER 4

1   Jennifer Amanda Jones, "Problems Migrate: Lessons from San Francisco's Homeless Population Survey," *Nonprofit Quarterly*, June 26, 2013, https://nonprofitquarterly.org/problems-migrate-lessons-from-san-francisco-s-homeless-population-survey.

2   Kerry Jackson and Wayne Winegarden, "San Francisco's Homeless Crisis: How Policy Reforms and Private Charities Can Move More People to Self-Sufficiency," Pacific Research Institute, 2019.

3   Kerry Jackson, "Criminal Justice Policy in SF Upside Down Under New SF District Attorney," *Right By the Bay*, Pacific Research Institute, April 15, 2020.

4   Heather Mac Donald, "San Francisco, Hostage to the Homeless," *City Journal*, Autumn 2019, https://www.city-journal.org/san-francisco-homelessness.

5   Michael Shellenberger, "Why California Keeps Making Homelessness Worse," *Forbes*, September 12, 2019, https://www.forbes.com/sites/michaelshellenberger/2019/09/12/why-california-keeps-making-homelessness-worse.

6   "The State of Homelessness in America," Council of Economic Advisors, September 2019.

7   Katy Grimes, "Will $1 Billion Spending on California's Homeless Fix the Problem?," *California Globe*, May 14, 2019, https://californiaglobe.com/fr/will-1-billion-spending-on-californias-homeless-fix-the-problem.

8   "6,686: A Civic Disgrace," *San Francisco Chronicle*, July 3, 2016, https://projects.sfchronicle.com/sf-homeless/civic-disgrace.

9   Mac Donald, "Hostage to the Homeless."

10 Mac Donald, "Hostage to the Homeless."

11 Devon Link, "Fact Check: San Francisco Providing Drugs, Alcohol to Quarantining Homeless but Not on Taxpayers' Dime," *USA Today*, May 13, 2020, https://www.usatoday.com/story/news/factcheck/2020/05/13/fact-check-san-francisco-project-room-key-provides-alcohol-tobacco/3111155001.

12 Dominic Fracassa and Kevin Fagan, "SF Gives Methadone, Alcohol, Cannabis to Some Addicts and Homeless Isolating from Coronavirus in Hotels," *San Francisco Chronicle*, May 8, 2020, https://www.sfchronicle.com/bayarea/article/SF-providing-medications-alcohol-cannabis-to-15251350.php.

13 Community Behavioral Health Services, Harm Reduction Policy, San Francisco Department of Public Health, https://www.sfdph.org/dph/comupg/oservices/mentalHlth/SubstanceAbuse/HarmReduction/default.asp#:~:text=Harm%20reduction%20is%20a%20public,on%20individuals%20and%20their%20community.

14 Erica Sandberg, "Harm Production in San Francisco," *City Journal*, February 14, 2019, https://www.city-journal.org/san-francisco-drugs-harm-reduction.

15 Erica Sandberg, "Free Booze, Pot, and Smokes for San Francisco's Homeless," *City Journal*, May 11, 2020, https://www.city-journal.org/san-francisco-homeless-free-alcohol-pot-cigarettes.

16 Kerry Jackson, "Opinion: California Leads the Nation in Bringing Back Medieval Illnesses," *Daily Caller*, March 21, 2019, https://dailycaller.com/2019/03/21/jackson-california-illness.

17 Mac Donald, "Hostage to the Homeless."

18 Joel John Roberts, "Is There a Homeless Industrial Complex That Perpetuates Homelessness?," *Poverty Insights*, August 5, 2013, http://www.povertyinsights.org/2013/08/05/is-there-a-homeless-industrial-complex-that-perpetuates-homelessness.

19 Roberts, "Is There a Homeless Industrial Complex?"

20 Roberts, "Is There a Homeless Industrial Complex?"

21 Carey Fuller, "The Homeless Industrial Complex Problem," *Huffington Post*, January 27, 2017, https://www.huffpost.com/entry/the-homeless-industrial-c_b_9092426.

22 Kenneth S. Alpern, "Finally! An Alternative to the Homeless Industrial Complex!," *CityWatch*, September 23, 2019, https://www.citywatchla.com/index.php/cw/los-angeles/18502-finally-an-alternative-to-the-homeless-industrial-complex.

23   Edward Ring, "How the Homeless Industrial Complex Plans to Destroy Ven-
     ice Beach," *California Globe*, April 22, 2020, https://californiaglobe.com/
     section-2/how-the-homeless-industrial-complex-plans-to-destroy-
     venice-beach.
24   Erica Sandberg, "San Francisco's False Solution," *City Journal*, October 10,
     2019.
25   Roberts, "Is There a Homeless Industrial Complex?"

CHAPTER 5

1   "NYT | Thousands of New Millionaires Are About to Eat San Francisco Alive,"
     Quartz, accessed May 12, 2020, https://qz.com/co/2324230/thousands-of-
     new-millionaires-are-about-to-eat-san-francisco-alive (link no longer avail-
     able); "SFDPH Mental Health Reform, Homelessness and Behavioral Health,
     Health Commission," San Francisco Health Network: San Francisco Depart-
     ment of Public Health, November 5, 2019, https://www.sfdph.org/dph/hc/
     HCAgen/2019/November%205/MH%20Reform_Health%20Commission%20
     11.5.19%20FINAL.pdf.
2   "Public Safety, Homelessness and Affordability Are Biggest Issues in 2018 SF
     Chamber Poll," San Francisco Chamber of Commerce, February 2, 2018,
     https://sfchamber.com/public-safety-homelessness-affordability-biggest-
     issues-2018-sf-chamber-poll; San Francisco Department of Public Health,
     San Francisco Methamphetamine Task Force: Final Report 2019, https://www.
     sfdph.org/dph/files/MethTaskForce/Meth%20Task%20Force%20Final%20
     Report_FULL.pdf.
3   "Adults Experiencing Homelessness, Psychosis and Substance Abuse Disor-
     der in San Francisco in FY2018–2019," Department of Public Health and/or
     Department of Homelessness and Supportive Housing, accessed May 12,
     2020, https://drive.google.com/file/d/15DX2lldi99xS847hxDJgXxEoLn
     UyKioJ/view?usp=sharing.
4   "Performance Audit of the Department of Public Health Behavioral Health
     Services," San Francisco Budget and Legislative Analyst, April 19, 2020,
     p. 149, https://sfbos.org/sites/default/files/041918_SF_MA_Behavioral_
     Health_Services.pdf.
5   Smita Das, Sebastien C. Fromont, and Judith J. Prochaska, "Bus Therapy:
     A Problematic Practice in Psychiatry," *JAMA Psychiatry* 70, No. 11 (November
     2013): 1127–1128, https://doi.org/10.1001/jamapsychiatry.2013.2824.
6   "Incarceration Is a Public Health Issue," Health Commission City and County
     of San Francisco, March 19, 2019, https://pretermbirthca.ucsf.edu/sites/g/
     files/tkssra2851/f/wysiwyg/IncarcerationisPublicHealthIssue.pdf.
7   Dale E. McNiel, Renée L. Binder, and Jo C. Robinson, "Incarceration Associ-
     ated with Homelessness, Mental Disorder, and Co-Occurring Substance
     Abuse," *Psychiatric Services* (Washington, D.C.) 56, No. 7 (July 2005): 840–
     846, https://doi.org/10.1176/appi.ps.56.7.840.

8   "SFDPH Mental Health Reform, Homelessness and Behavioral Health, Health Commission."

9   "Fiscal Year 2019–2020 and 2020–2021 Budget, Local Homeless Coordinating Board," Department of Homelessness and Supportive Housing, July 1, 2019, http://hsh.sfgov.org/wp-content/uploads/2019-HSH-Budget-Presentation-for-LHCB_07.01.19.pdf; "Performance Audit of the City's Assumption of the San Francisco Housing Authority's Essential Functions," San Francisco Budget and Legislative Analyst, September 9, 2019, https://sfbos.org/sites/default/files/BLA.PerformanceAudit_SFHousingAuthority.pdf.

10   "Bay Area Homelessness: A Regional View of a Regional Crisis," Bay Area Council Economic Institute, April 2019, http://www.bayareaeconomy.org/report/bay-area-homelessness.

11   "SF Mayor Breed, Supervisors Agree on Plan to Overhaul City's Mental Health Program," KQED, November 12, 2019, https://www.kqed.org/news/11786202/s-f-mayor-breed-and-supes-agree-on-plan-to-overhaul-citys-mental-health-program.

12   "2019 San Francisco Homeless Count & Survey Comprehensive Report," Applied Survey Research, 2019, accessed May 12, 2020, https://hsh.sfgov.org/wp-content/uploads/2020/01/2019HIRDReport_SanFrancisco_FinalDraft-1.pdf.

13   Heather Carroll, "Serious Mental Illness and Anosognosia," Treatment Advocacy Center, accessed May 12, 2020, https://www.treatmentadvocacy-center.org/key-issues/anosognosia/3628-serious-mental-illness-and-anosognosia.

14   E. Fuller Torrey, Kurt Entsminger, Jeffrey Geller, Jonathan Stanley, and D. J. Jaffe, "The Shortage of Public Hospital Beds for Mentally Ill Persons," Treatment Advocacy Center, n.d., 17.

15   "California's Acute Psychiatric Bed Loss," California Hospital Association, March 28, 2018, p. 14, https://www.calhospital.org/sites/main/files/file-attachments/psychbeddata.pdf.

16   Ida Mojadad, "San Francisco Weighs Corruption Reform – Will It Work?," *SF Weekly*, February 13, 2020, https://www.sfweekly.com/news/san-francisco-corruption-reform; Trisha Thadani, "SF Could Compel More Severely Mentally Ill People into Treatment under Law," *San Francisco Chronicle*, October 3, 2019, https://www.sfchronicle.com/politics/article/SF-may-compel-more-severely-mentally-ill-people-14487044.php.

17   Channon Gafford, "Bart Station Junkies Taking Over! Part 3," YouTube, April 28, 2018, https://www.youtube.com/watch?v=8fr9A4ZDxCg&feature=emb_title.

18   Christopher F. Rufo, "Our system is broken," Facebook, December 27, 2019, https://www.facebook.com/realchrisrufo/posts/our-system-is-broken-last-month-a-citizen-reported-a-homeless-woman-eating-a-dea/506044786684112.

Notes

19 Chesa Boudin 博徹思 (@ChesaBoudin), "Here is a clip of @shaunking speaking to the crowd," Twitter, November 23, 2019, https://twitter.com/chesaboudin/status/1198389603415146496; "Boudin Will Not Prosecute Prostitution, Public Camping, and Other 'Quality-of-Life Crimes' Once Sworn In," SFist, November 16, 2019, https://sfist.com/2019/11/16/boudin-will-not-prosecute-prostitution-public-camping-and-other-quality-of-life-crimes-once-sworn-in.

20 Meagan Day, "Chesa Boudin Wants to Transform San Francisco's Criminal Justice System," *Jacobin*, May 2019, https://jacobinmag.com/2019/05/chesa-boudin-san-francisco-district-attorney.

21 "Ending Mass Incarceration," Chesa Boudin District Attorney 2019, accessed May 12, 2020, https://web.archive.org/web/20191219154342/https://www.chesaboudin.com/mass_incarceration.

22 "The San Francisco County Jails," San Francisco Sheriff, April 8, 2016, https://www.sfdph.org/dph/files/jrp/WG-MeetingCombined.pdf.

23 "Adults Experiencing Homelessness, Psychosis and Substance Abuse Disorder."

24 Erica Sandberg, "San Francisco's Quality-of-Life Toll," *City Journal*, May 19, 2019, https://www.city-journal.org/san-francisco-crime; Phil Matier, "In SF's Tenderloin, There's a Revolving Door – of Drug Dealers, That Is," *San Francisco Chronicle*, May 12, 2019, https://www.sfchronicle.com/bayarea/philmatier/article/In-SF-s-Tenderloin-there-s-a-revolving-door-13836919.php.

25 "What America's Users Spend on Illegal Drugs: 2000–2010," RAND Corporation, February 2014, https://obamawhitehouse.archives.gov/sites/default/files/ondcp/policy-and-research/wausid_results_report.pdf; "2019 San Francisco Homeless Count & Survey, Comprehensive Report."

26 Katie Canales, "San Francisco Car Break-Ins Are so Common That the City's District Attorney Is Proposing Reimbursing Residents Whose Windows Are Smashed," *Business Insider*, February 13, 2020, https://www.businessinsider.com/san-francisco-is-proposing-reimbursing-car-break-in-victims-2020-2.

27 Alex Savidge (@AlexSavidgeKTVU), "COMPENSATING VICTIMS: San Francisco District Attorney Chesa Boudin Is Seeking $1.5 Million in His Budget," Twitter, February 12, 2020, https://twitter.com/alexsavidgektvu/status/1227739206409043968.

28 "6,686: A Civic Disgrace."

29 Dominic Fracassa, "For SF Meth Users, a Sobering Center Is Planned. What Would That Look Like?," *San Francisco Chronicle*, October 26, 2019, https://www.sfchronicle.com/bayarea/article/For-SF-meth-users-a-sobering-center-is-planned-14563728.php.

30 Evan Sernoffsky and John King, "Fentanyl, Heroin Overdoses in San Francisco More than Doubled in 2019," *San Francisco Chronicle*, January 21, 2020, https://www.sfchronicle.com/bayarea/article/Fentanyl-heroin-overdoses-in-San-Francisco-more-14993628.php.

31 Das, Fromont, and Prochaska, "Bus Therapy."

32 SF Department of Public Health, *San Francisco Methamphetamine Task Force*.

33 SF Department of Public Health, *San Francisco Methamphetamine Task Force*, 42.

34 SF Department of Public Health, *San Francisco Methamphetamine Task Force*, 17, 19, 12, 23.

35 "Adults Experiencing Homelessness, Psychosis and Substance Abuse Disorder."

36 Alex Berezow, "City of San Francisco Pays for Billboard on 'Safe' Heroin Injection," American Council on Science and Health, August 27, 2020, https://www.acsh.org/news/2020/08/27/city-san-francisco-pays-billboard-safe-heroin-injection-14994.

37 homelessphilosopher, "'Streets of San Francisco' on Twitter," *Homelessphilosopher* (blog), August 21, 2019, https://homelessphilosopher.wordpress.com/2019/08/21/streets-of-san-francisco-on-twitter.

38 Joshua Sabatini, "In Inaugural Speech, Breed Focuses on 'Twin Troubles' of Homelessness, Affordable Housing," *San Francisco Examiner*, January 8, 2020,https://www.sfexaminer.com/news/in-inaugural-speech-breed-focuses-on-twin-troubles-of-homelessness-affordable-housing.

39 Joan Didion, *Slouching Towards Bethlehem* (Seattle: Burning Man Books, 1967), 5–35, https://nstearns.edublogs.org/files/2012/03/Slouching-toward-bethlehem-184kxww.pdf.

CHAPTER **6**

1   Homeless advocacy groups often cite poverty and cost of living as important contributors to homelessness. See, for example, "Homelessness in America," National Coalition for the Homeless, accessed June 10, 2020, https://nationalhomeless.org/about-homelessness.

2   See "Cost of Living," Federal Reserve Bank of St. Louis, accessed June 17, 2020, https://research.stlouisfed.org/publications/cost-of-living/calculator.

3   See US Census income tables, accessed June 17, 2020, https://www.census.gov/topics/income-poverty/income.html.

4   "2020 State of Salaries Report: Salary Benchmarks and Talent Preferences," Hired.com, 2020, https://hired.com/blog/highlights/2020-state-of-salaries-report.

5   "2020 State of Salaries Report."

6   "2020 State of Salaries Report."

7   Lauren Monitz, "How Much You Need to Live Comfortably in 50 Major US Cities," GoBankingRates.com, December 20, 2018, https://www.msn.com/en-us/money/personalfinance/heres-the-cost-of-living-in-americas-50-biggest-cities/ss-BBO31aU#image=51.

8   Monitz, "How Much You Need."

9   Monitz, "How Much You Need."

10 Monitz, "How Much You Need."

11 "Quarter 1, 2020 Cost of Living Index Released," Council for Community and Economic Research, May 2020, http://coli.org/quarter-1-2019-cost-of-living-index-released-3.

Notes

12   Scott Cohn, "America's 10 Most Expensive States to Live in 2019," CNBC, July 10, 2019, https://www.cnbc.com/2019/07/10/americas-10-most-expensive-states-to-live-in-2019.html.

13   "Affordability Rankings," *U.S. News & World Report*, accessed June 23, 2020, https://www.usnews.com/news/best-states/rankings/opportunity/affordability.

14   "Cost of Living Index by State 2020," *World Population Review*, accessed June 23, 2020, https://worldpopulationreview.com/states/cost-of-living-index-by-state.

15   "The Supplemental Poverty Measure: 2018," US Census Bureau, October 2019, https://www.census.gov/content/dam/Census/library/publications/2019/demo/p60-268.pdf.

16   "Population and Housing Unit Estimates," US Census Bureau, accessed September 21, 2020, https://www.census.gov/programs-surveys/popest.html.

17   See, for instance, "Rental Burdens: Rethinking Affordability Measures," US Department of Housing and Urban Development, *PD&R Edge*, September 2014, https://www.huduser.gov/portal/pdredge/pdr_edge_featd_article_092214.html.

18   Median household income data are from the US Census: https://www.census.gov/topics/income-poverty/income.html.

19   The median home price in California and California regions are from the California Association of Realtors (https://car.sharefile.com/share/view/soc02663a5c54e23a, accessed July 2020). US median existing home price is from the US Census Bureau.

20   The average annual interest rate on a 30-year mortgage for each year is from the St. Louis Fed, FRED system: https://fred.stlouisfed.org/index.html.

21   "State Electricity Profiles," US Energy Information Administration, various years, https://www.eia.gov/electricity/state.

22   "2020 Electricity Rates by State," Payless Power, April 2020, https://paylesspower.com/blog/electric-rates-by-state.

23   See "State Gas Price Averages," AAA prices as of June 17, 2020, https://gasprices.aaa.com/state-gas-price-averages.

24   "Weekly Retail Gasoline and Diesel Prices," US Energy Information Administration, https://www.eia.gov/dnav/pet/pet_pri_gnd_a_epmr_pte_dpgal_a.htm.

25   "US States' Grocery Prices Ranked from Most Expensive to Cheapest," LoveMoney.com, February 27, 2019, https://www.lovemoney.com/gallerylist/82342/us-states-grocery-prices-ranked-from-most-expensive-to-cheapest.

26   "San Francisco 2017 Homeless Count & Survey: Comprehensive Report," Applied Survey Research, 2017.

27   "Causes & Solutions to Homelessness," LA Family Housing, accessed June 23, 2020, https://lafh.org/causes-solutions.

28   "The Mayors' 2020 Vision for America: A Call to Action Make Housing More Affordable and End Homelessness," United States Conference of Mayors,

https://www.usmayors.org/2020-vision/make-housing-more-affordable-and-end-homelessness (emphasis added).

29 "Homelessness in America: Overview of Data and Causes," National Law Center on Homelessness and Poverty, January 2015, https://nlchp.org/wp-content/uploads/2018/10/Homeless_Stats_Fact_Sheet.pdf.

30 Matt Levin and Jackie Botts, "California's Homelessness Crisis – and Possible Solutions – Explained," CalMatters, December 31, 2019, https://calmatters.org/explainers/californias-homelessness-crisis-explained.

CHAPTER 7

1   See, e.g., Alicia da Rado, "Legal Warriors in Battle Over City's Homeless: Attorneys Harry Simon and Robert Wheeler Line Up on Opposite Sides in the Dispute Over Laws Governing the Homeless in Santa Ana," *Los Angeles Times*, January 30, 1994 ("'These laws make being poor a criminal act,' says Simon, 32, who has put countless hours into defending the rights of the homeless in civil court. Then Wheeler, 52, takes his turn: 'The city has an obligation to everyone in Orange County to make the Civic Center open, accessible and safe.' So goes the war of words in Santa Ana's ongoing fight to outlaw the homeless from sleeping on the city's streets.").

2   *Joyce v. City & Cty. of San Francisco*, 846 F. Supp. 843 (N.D. Cal. 1994) (Munger, Tolles & Olson LLP); *Streetwatch v. Nat'l R.R. Passenger Corp.*, 875 F. Supp. 1055 (S.D.N.Y. 1995) (Yale Law clinic); *In re Eichorn*, 69 Cal. App. 4th 382, 384 (1998) (O'Melveny & Myers LLP); *Betancourt v. Bloomberg*, 448 F. 3d 547, 553 (2d Cir. 2006) (Paul, Weiss, Rifkind, Wharton & Garrison LLP); *Martin v. City of Boise*, No. 1:09-cv-00540-REB, 2015 WL 5708586 (D. Idaho Sept. 28, 2015) (Latham & Watkins LLP).

3   National Law Center on Homelessness and Poverty [now National Homelessness Law Center], *No Safe Place: The Criminalization of Homelessness in U.S. Cities* (date unclear, probably 2014), 18.

4   L.A. Municipal Code section 41.18(d).

5   *Jones v. City of Los Angeles*, 444 F. 3d 1118 (9th Cir. 2006), *vacated by* 505 F. 3d 1006 (9th Cir. 2007). The appellants, notably, sought only relief from enforcement of the ordinance during nighttime hours, i.e., between 9:00 P.M. and 6:30 A.M., or at any time against the temporarily infirm or permanently disabled.

6   *Id.* at 1136.

7   Randal C. Archibold, "Los Angeles to Permit Sleeping on Sidewalks," *New York Times*, October 11, 2007, https://www.nytimes.com/2007/10/11/us/11skidrow.html.

8   The panel decision issued in September 2018; the en banc decision was in April 2019.

9   A disorderly conduct ordinance was also challenged but I focus on the camping ordinance for simplicity's sake.

Notes

10   *Martin v. City of Boise*, 920 F. 3d 584, 618 (9th Cir. 2019).

11   *Martin*, 920 F. 3d at 617. The panel relied on two US Supreme Court decisions from the 1960s. One case, *Robinson v. California*, 370 U.S. 660 (1962), struck down a California law that punished a person for being a drug "addict." In the second case, *Powell v. Texas*, 392 U.S. 514 (1968), Justice Thurgood Marshall, for a plurality of the court, upheld a statute outlawing public drunkenness. Together the two cases hold that a government cannot punish a "status," like addiction, but that it can punish behavior that threatens public health and safety, like being drunk in public.

12   *Martin*, 920 F. 3d at 599 (Smith, J., dissenting from the denial of rehearing en banc).

13   *Martin*, 920 F. 3d at 596 (Smith, J., dissenting from the denial of rehearing en banc).

14   *Martin*, 920 F. 3d at 618.

15   *Martin v. City of Boise*, Case No. 1:09-cv-540-REB, Doc. 78, at 5. Officers testified that they issued tickets only when it was clear that an individual was doing more than simply sleeping in public.

16   *See, e.g., In re Eichorn*, 69 Cal. App. 4th 382, 384 (1998) (legal defense of necessity exist for defendants charged with quality-of-life crimes, in that case public camping).

17   *See, e.g., Frank v. City of St. Louis*, No. 4:20-cv-00597-SEP, 2020 WL 2116392, at *4 (E.D. Mo. May 2, 2020) (St. Louis could close a downtown encampment, at least during the COVID-19 pandemic, in part because there is no evidence that "[the homeless plaintiff] faces a genuine threat of criminal punishment"); *Young v. City of Los Angeles*, No. 20-cv-709-JFW-RAO, 2020 WL 616363, at *5 (C.D. Cal. Feb. 10, 2020) (*Martin* covers only "criminally prosecuting" homeless individuals); *Winslow v. City of Oakland*, No. 20-cv-01510-CRB, 2020 WL 1031759, at *4 (N.D. Cal. Mar. 3, 2020) ("while *Martin* limits localities' ability to arrest their homeless residents for the act of living in the streets when there is nowhere else for them to go, it does not create a right for homeless residents to occupy indefinitely any public space of their choosing"); *Hous. Is a Human Right Orange Cty. v. Cty. of Orange*, No. 19-cv-388-PAJ-DEX, 2019 WL 8012374, at *5 (C.D. Cal. Oct. 28, 2019) (*Martin* only applies with "the initiation of the criminal process"); *Quintero v. City of Santa Cruz*, No. 5:19-cv-01898-EJD, 2019 WL 1924990, at *1 (N.D. Cal. Apr. 30, 2019) (Martin does not apply where there are no prosecutions); *Le Van Hung v. Schaaf*, No. 19-cv-01436-CRB, 2019 WL 1779584, at *1 (N.D. Cal. Apr. 23, 2019) (a "clear and clean" operation does not implicate *Martin* since such a sweep does not require the arrest of plaintiffs); *Shipp v. Schaaf*, No. 19-cv-01709-JST, 2019 WL 1644401, at *1 (N.D. Cal. Apr. 16, 2019) (*Martin* claim rejected because Oakland only required temporary vacation of the encampment and this effort by itself did not implicate criminal sanctions); *Butcher v. City of Marysville*, No. 2:18-cv-2765-JAM-CKD, 2019 WL 918203, at *1 (E.D. Cal. Feb. 25, 2019) (*Martin* claim could not proceed,

because, although two plaintiffs had been threatened with arrest, the threat came not pursuant to enforcement of a criminal ordinance but to evacuate a flooded area – a public health and safety reason). *See also State v. Barrett*, 302 Or. App. 23, 30 (2020) (judges of the Court of Appeals of Oregon differing on the *Martin* question). For other cases under the Eighth Amendment, *see Miralle v. City of Oakland*, No. 18-cv-06823-HSG, 2018 WL 6199929, at *2 (N.D. Cal. Nov. 28, 2018); *Sullivan v. City of Berkeley*, No. 17-cv-06051 WHA, 2017 WL 4922614, at *3 (N.D. Cal. Oct. 31, 2017); *Nishi v. Cty. of Marin*, No. 11-cv-0438 PJH, 2012 WL 566408, at *7 (N.D. Cal. Feb. 21, 2012); *Sanchez v. City of Fresno*, 914 F. Supp. 2d 1079, 1109 (E.D. Cal. 2012); *Pottinger v. City of Miami*, 810 F. Supp. 1551, 1580 (S.D. Fla. 1992).

18 *Aitken v. City of Aberdeen*, No. 3:19-cv-05322-RBL, 2019 WL 2764423, at *1 (W.D. Wash. July 2, 2019).
19 *Blake v. City of Grants Pass*, No. 1:18-cv-01823-CL, 2020 WL 4209227, at *1 (D. Or. July 22, 2020).
20 *Grants Pass*, 2019 WL 3717800, at *8.
21 *Mahoney v. City of Sacramento*, No. 2:20-cv-0258-KJM-CKD, 2020 WL 616302, at *3 (E.D. Cal. Feb. 10, 2020).
22 *See, e.g.*, San Francisco Police Code Sec. 22(a); see also L.A. Municipal Code 41.18(a).
23 *Betancourt v. Bloomberg*, 448 F. 3d 547, 549–50 (2d Cir. 2006).
24 *Betancourt*, 448 F. 3d at 553.
25 *Betancourt*, 448 F.3 d at 560 (Calabresi, J., dissenting). A decade earlier, a Hawaiian plaintiff living in his van approximated one of Judge Calabresi's hypotheticals by claiming that his vehicle was his "mobile photography studio" and that he obtained his "inspiration moving around from one place to another" and took "a lot of night photographs." *Hawai'i v. Sturch*, 921 P.2d 1170, 1173 (Ct. App. Haw. 1996).
26 S.F. Police Code 169(c) & 169(b)(1).
27 S.F. Police Code 169(a)(2)-(3).
28 L.A. Municipal Code Sec. 41.18(d); Santa Monica Municipal Code § 3.12.360 & 4.08.097; Santa Cruz Municipal Code § 9.50.011-14 & 9.50.020.
29 *Roulette v. City of Seattle*, 97 F.3d 300, 302 (9th Cir. 1996).
30 *Roulette*, 97 F. 3d at 302 (ordinance's scope) & 304 (sitting or lying is not expression).
31 *Roulette*, 97 F. 3d at 315 (Norris, J., dissent respecting the denial of rehearing en banc).
32 *Roulette*, 97 F. 3d at 316 (Norris, J., dissent respecting the denial of rehearing en banc).
33 S.F. Police Code 168(a).
34 S.F. Police Code 168(b) & (c) (prohibition and exceptions); *id.* at 168(d) & (f) (warning and penalties); *id.* at 168(h) (social services).
35 S.F. Police Code 168(a).
36 S.F. Police Code 168(a).

Notes

37 Ted Andersen, "What Happened to SF's Controversial 'Sit-Lie' Ordinance?," *SF Gate*, October 18, 2018, https://www.sfgate.com/bayarea/article/What-happened-to-SF-s-controversial-sit-lie-13303216.php.

38 Heather Knight, "Sit/Lie Law Primarily Enforced in Haight," *SF Gate*, April 23, 2013, https://www.sfgate.com/news/article/Sit-lie-law-primarily-enforced-in-Haight-3763521.php.

39 *Lavan v. City of Los Angeles*, 693 F. 3d 1022, 1023–24 (9th Cir. 2012).

40 *Lavan*, 693 F. 3d at 1032.

41 *Lavan*, 693 F. 3d at 1033.

42 *Lavan*, 693 F. 3d at 1035 n.1 (Callahan, J., dissenting).

43 *Lavan*, 693 F. 3d at 1034–35 (Callahan, J., dissenting).

44 *Mitchell v. City of Los Angeles*, Case No. 2:16-cv-1750-SJO-JPR (C.D. Cal.), Doc. 119 (May 31, 2019). The terms of the settlement are at pp. 7–15.

45 Nick Bastone, "2 Years After Angry Silicon Valley Locals Chanted 'Build a Wall' to Keep the Homeless Out, Mountain View Is Reportedly Cracking Down on a Growing RV Camp Outside Google's HQ," *Business Insider*, May 22, 2019, https://www.businessinsider.com/silicon-valley-rv-residents-may-soon-be-forced-out-2019-5; Kiet Do, "Silicon Valley Homeless Population Spikes; RV Dwellers More Than Double," *CBS SF Bay Area*, July 15, 2019, https://sanfrancisco.cbslocal.com/2019/07/15/homeless-rv-dwellers-silicon-valley-santa-clara-county.

46 See, e.g., Associated Press, "San Francisco: More Homeless Living in Vehicles," *NBC Bay Area*, July 5, 2019, https://www.nbcbayarea.com/news/local/san-francisco-more-homeless-living-in-vehicles/172005.

47 Kevin Faulconer, "How San Diego Cleaned Up Its Act – And Got Real on Homelessness," *Hoover Institution*, October 30, 2019.

48 *Desertrain v. City of Los Angeles*, 754 F. 3d 1147, 1149, 1155–56 (9th Cir. 2014).

49 *Desertrain*, 754 F. 3d at 1157.

50 *Desertrain*, 754 F. 3d at 1157.

51 *Desertrain*, 754 F. 3d at 1157–58.

52 L.A. Mun. Code 85.02(A)(1)-(2).

53 L.A. Mun. Code 85.02(B)(2).

54 Emily Alpert Reyes, "L.A. City Council Votes to Reimpose Limits on Living in Vehicles," *Los Angeles Times*, July 30, 2019, https://www.latimes.com/california/story/2019-07-30/homeless-cars-la-law.

55 Anna Scott, "Amid Homelessness Crisis, Los Angeles Restricts Living in Vehicles," *NPR*, August 19, 2019, https://www.npr.org/2019/08/19/751802740/amid-homelessness-crisis-los-angeles-restricts-living-in-vehicles.

56 Scott, "Amid Homelessness Crisis."

57 *Young v. New York City Transit Auth.*, 903 F. 2d 146, 156 (2d Cir. 1990).

58 *Blair v. Shanahan*, 775 F. Supp. 1315, 1324 n.9 ("disturbing"), 1322–23 ("Begging gives the speaker") (N.D. Cal. 1991), *appeal dismissed and remanded*, 38 F. 3d 1514 (9th Cir. 1994), and *vacated*, 919 F. Supp. 1361 (N.D. Cal. 1996).

59 *Blair*, 775 F. Supp. 1315, 1325, *appeal dismissed and remanded*, 38 F. 3d 1514, and *vacated*, 919 F. Supp. 1361.

60 *Loper v. New York City Police Dep't*, 999 F. 2d 699, 704 (2d Cir. 1993). See also *Village of Schaumburg v. Citizens for a Better Environment*, et al., 44 U.S. 620 (1980).

61 *Loper*, 999 F. 2d at 704.

62 S.F. Police Code, Sec. 120-2(a).

63 S.F. Police Code, Sec. 120-2(c) [definitions], (d) [prohibitions], (e) [penalties].

64 Kevin Fagan, "New Panhandling Law – S.F. to Take It Easy/City Says It Will Use Persuasion, Not Jail," *SF Gate*, May 25, 2004, https://www.sfgate.com/news/article/New-panhandling-law-S-F-to-take-it-easy-2756122.php.

65 *Gresham v. Peterson*, 225 F. 3d 899, 903 (7th Cir. 2000).

66 *Gresham*, 225 F. 3d at 906.

67 *Heffron v. Int'l Soc. for Krishna Consciousness, Inc.*, 452 U.S. 640, 655 (1981); *Young v. New York City Transit Authority*, 903 F. 2d 146, 160 (2d Cir.); *Int'l Soc. for Krishna Consciousness, Inc. v. Lee*, 505 U.S. 672, 685 (1992).

68 *See, e.g.*, Robert Teir, "Maintaining Safety and Civility in Public Spaces: A Constitutional Approach to Aggressive Begging," *Louisiana Law Review* 54 (1993), https://digitalcommons.law.lsu.edu/lalrev/vol54/iss2/3; George F. Will, "Beggars and Judicial Imperialism," *Washington Post*, February 1, 1990 ("The question of what society owes in compassionate help to street people is, surely, severable from the question of what right the community has to protect a minimally civilized ambience in public spaces.... [S]uch behavior (panhandling, public drunkenness, prostitution, pornographic displays) can destroy a community faster than a gang of professional burglars.")

69 Rachel Swan, "Panhandling Ban Gets Nod from BART Lawyers, but Debate Rages Among Directors," *San Francisco Chronicle*, October 23, 2019, https://www.sfchronicle.com/bayarea/article/Panhandling-ban-gets-nod-from-BART-lawyers-but-14551646.php.

70 *Evans v. Sandy City*, 944 F. 3d 847, 851 (10th Cir. 2019).

71 *Evans*, 944 F. 3d at 854–55; *id.* at 861 (Briscoe, J., dissenting).

72 S.F. Health Code, Sec. 581(b)(1) & (5).

CHAPTER 8

1 Terrence McCoy, "Meet the Outsider Who Accidentally Solved Chronic Homelessness," *Washington Post*, May 12, 2020, https://www.washingtonpost.com/news/inspired-life/wp/2015/05/06/meet-the-outsider-who-accidentally-solved-chronic-homelessness.

2 Matt Levin and Jackie Botts, "How Many People Are Homeless?," CalMatters, December 31, 2019.

3 "'We Need to Have an Entitlement to Housing': L.A. Mayor Eric Garcetti on Homelessness," *KTLA 5*, January 9, 2020, https://www.youtube.com/watch?v=C-bm9YeaK9l.

Notes

4   Gavin Newsom (@GavinNewsom), "Doctors should be able to write pre-scriptions for housing the same way they do for insulin or antibiotics," Twitter, February 21, 2020, https://twitter.com/gavinnewsom/status/1230889348167434240.

5   "2019 AHAR: Part 1 – PIT Estimates of Homelessness in the U.S.," HUD Exchange, January 2020, https://www.hudexchange.info/resource/5948/2019-ahar-part-1-pit-estimates-of-homelessness-in-the-us.

6   "Los Angeles, California, Homelessness Reduction and Prevention Housing, and Facilities Bond Issue, Measure HHH (November 2016)," Ballotpedia, accessed May 12, 2020, https://ballotpedia.org/Los_Angeles,_California,_Homelessness_Reduction_and_Prevention_Housing,_and_Facilities_Bond_Issue,_Measure_HHH_(November_2016).

7   Rachel Uranga, "FBI Probe of Councilman Huizar Widens | Lawsuit Seeks to Block Boyle Heights Charter School | Focus on Sunset Junction Style," East-sider LA, January 14, 2019, https://www.theeastsiderla.com/news/news_notes/fbi-probe-of-councilman-huizar-widens-lawsuit-seeks-to-block-boyle-heights-charter-school-focus/article_5441eddc-db57-597b-a4f8-6e999676808c.html.

8   "The High Cost of Homeless Housing: Review of Proposition HHH," Los Angeles City Controller Ron Galperin, October 8, 2019, https://lacontroller.org/audits-and-reports/high-cost-of-homeless-housing-hhh.

9   "Data," Los Angeles Homeless Services Authority, accessed May 12, 2020, https://www.lahsa.org/data?id=13-2019-homeless-count-by-community-city.

10 Joe Donatelli, "Your Cheat Sheet for the 6 Local Issues on the Ballot Tomorrow," Los Angeles Magazine (blog), October 7, 2016, https://www.lamag.com/culturefiles/los-angeles-ballot-measures-2016; Gwynedd Stuart, "Will a Measure to Help L.A.'s Homeless Become a Historic Public Housing Debacle?," Los Angeles Magazine (blog), March 8, 2019, https://www.lamag.com/citythinkblog/proposition-hhh-debacle.

11 Gwynedd Stuart, "An Audit Lays Out What's Gone Wrong with L.A.'s Home-less Housing Measure," Los Angeles Magazine (blog), October 10, 2019, https://www.lamag.com/citythinkblog/proposition-hhh-audit.

12 Benjamin Oreskes and Doug Smith, "Homelessness Jumped 13% in L.A. County, 14% in the City Before Pandemic," Los Angeles Times, June 12, 2020, https://www.latimes.com/homeless-housing/story/2020-06-12/la-homelessness-jumped-before-coronavirus-hit.

13 Mary E. Larimer, Daniel K. Malone, Michelle D. Garner, et al., "Health Care and Public Service Use and Costs Before and After Provision of Housing for Chronically Homeless Persons with Severe Alcohol Problems," JAMA 301, No. 13 (April 1, 2009): 1349–1357, https://doi.org/10.1001/jama.2009.414; "The Applicability of Housing First Models to Homeless Persons with Serious Mental Illness," HUD USER, accessed May 12, 2020, https://www.huduser.gov/portal/publications/homeless/hsgfirst.html; Kelly McEvers, "Utah

Reduced Chronic Homelessness By 91 Percent; Here's How," NPR, December 10, 2015, https://www.npr.org/2015/12/10/459100751/utah-reduced-chronic-homelessness-by-91-percent-heres-how.

14 Larimer et al., "Health Care and Public Service."

15 "The Homeless Homed," *Daily Show with Jon Stewart*, January 7, 2015, http://www.cc.com/shows/the-daily-show-with-jon-stewart/cast/cd00ef65-8df8-407b-8438-2b23cb64a582/lntv3q/the-homeless-homed; "Utah Is Winning the War on Chronic Homelessness with 'Housing First' Program," *Los Angeles Times*, May 24, 2015, https://www.latimes.com/nation/la-na-utah-housing-first-20150524-story.html; McEvers, "Utah Reduced Chronic Homelessness."

16 Eric Schulzke, "Is Utah Still a Model for Solving Chronic Homelessness?," *Deseret News*, April 27, 2017, https://www.deseret.com/2017/4/28/20611325/is-utah-still-a-model-for-solving-chronic-homelessness.

17 Gregory Scruggs, "Once a National Model, Utah Struggles with Homelessness," Reuters, January 10, 2019, https://www.reuters.com/article/us-usa-homelessness-housing-idUSKCN1P41EQ.

18 McCoy, "Meet the Outsider."

19 Janey Rountree, Nathan Hess, and Austin Lyke, "Health Conditions Among Unsheltered Adults in the U.S.," Policy Brief, California Policy Lab, October 2019, p. 9.

20 Sam Tsemberis, Leyla Gulcur, and Maria Nakae, "Housing First, Consumer Choice, and Harm Reduction for Homeless Individuals with a Dual Diagnosis," *American Journal of Public Health* 94, No. 4 (April 1, 2004): 651–656, https://doi.org/10.2105/AJPH.94.4.651.mentally ill individuals' on those individuals' consumer choice, housing stability, substance use, treatment utilization, and psychiatric symptoms. Methods. Two hundred twenty-five participants were randomly assigned to receive housing contingent on treatment and sobriety (control

21 Carol Pearson, Ann Elizabeth Montgomery, and Gretchen Locke, "Housing Stability among Homeless Individuals with Serious Mental Illness Participating in Housing First Programs," *Journal of Community Psychology* 37, No. 3 (2009): 404–417, https://doi.org/10.1002/jcop.20303.

22 Rebecca A. Cherner, Tim Aubry, John Sylvestre, Rob Boyd, and Donna Pettey, "Housing First for Adults with Problematic Substance Use," *Journal of Dual Diagnosis* 13, No. 3 (September 2017): 219–229, https://doi.org/10.1080/15504263.2017.1319586.

23 Stefan G. Kertesz, Kimberly Crouch, Jesse B. Milby, Robert E. Cusimano, and Joseph E. Schumacher, "Housing First for Homeless Persons with Active Addiction: Are We Overreaching?," *Milbank Quarterly* 87, No. 2 (June 2009): 495–534, https://doi.org/10.1111/j.1468-0009.2009.00565.x., pp. 522–523.

24 Kertesz et al., "Housing First for Homeless Persons," 523.

25 Cherner et al., "Housing First for Adults."

26 Kertesz et al., "Housing First for Homeless Persons," 497.

27 "The Applicability of Housing First Models to Homeless Persons with Serious

Notes

Mental Illness," HUD USER, accessed May 12, 2020, https://www.huduser. gov/portal/publications/homeless/hsgfirst.html, p. 35.

28 Victoria Stanhope and Kerry Dunn, "The Curious Case of Housing First: The Limits of Evidence Based Policy," *International Journal of Law and Psychiatry* 34, no. 4 (August 2011): 275–282, https://doi.org/10.1016/j.ijlp.2011.07.006.

29 "Study Suggests 'Housing First' Model Worsens Homelessness," *NBC Los Angeles* (blog), February 21, 2020, https://www.nbclosangeles.com/news/ local/streets-of-shame/study-suggests-housing-first-model-worsens-homelessness/2313300.

30 Stefan G. Kertesz and Saul J. Weiner, "Housing the Chronically Homeless: High Hopes, Complex Realities," *JAMA* 301, No. 17 (May 6, 2009): 1822–1824, https://doi.org/10.1001/jama.2009.596.

CHAPTER 9

1 *Housing Is a Human Right Orange County, et al. v. County of Orange, et al.*, Case No. 8:19-cv-00388-PA-JDE, Doc. 79 (July 5, 2019), at 3.

2 Nick Gerda, "Homeless Settlement Limits South County Anti-Camping Enforcement," *Voice of OC*, July 23, 2019, https://voiceofoc.org/2019/07/ homeless-settlement-limits-south-county-anti-camping-enforcement.

3 *Orange County Catholic Worker v. Orange County*, Case No. 8:18-cv-00155-DOC-JDE, Doc. 318-1 (July 23, 2019), at section 4.1 (anti-camping), 4.3 (warning and enforcement), 5 (Collaborative Court), 6 (clean ups), 8 (clinical assessments), 10 (due process). *See also* Luke Money, Faith E. Pinho, Hillary Davis, and Priscella Vega, "Unsheltered, Part 2: Once Reluctant, These Orange County Cities Are Opening Homeless Shelters," *Los Angeles Times*, December 31, 2019, https://www.latimes.com/california/story/2019-12-31/ homeless-orange-county-unsheltered-series-part-2. *Orange County Catholic Worker v. Orange County*, Case No. 8:18-cv-00155-DOC-JDE, Doc. 318-1 (July 23, 2019). The text of the *Catholic Worker* settlement is available here: https://voiceofoc.org/wp-content/uploads/2019/07/County-settlement-agreement-in-homelessness-lawsuit-July-2019.pdf.

4 UC Hastings, "Tenderloin Settlement Agreement: Updates and Progress," June 30, 2020, https://www.uchastings.edu/2020/06/30/tenderloin-settlement-agreement.

5 Heather Knight, "Tenderloin Tents Are Now Rare. Open-Air Drug Dealing Is Still All Too Common," *S.F. Chronicle*, September 5, 2020, https://www. sfchronicle.com/bayarea/heatherknight/article/Tenderloin-tents-are-now-rare-Open-air-drug-15544410.php#photo-19914263.

6 Theresa Walker, "With Judge Carter Out in Key Case, How Will Homeless Lawsuits Work in Orange County?," *Orange County Register*, June 21, 2019, https://www.ocregister.com/2019/06/21/with-judge-carter-out-how-will-homeless-lawsuits-work-in-orange-county; Jones Day, "Orange County Cities Obtain Dismissal of Putative Class Claims Relating to Response to Homelessness Epidemic," August 2019, https://www.jonesday.com/en/

practices/experience/2019/08/orange-county-cities-obtain-dismissal-of-putative.

7   *L.A. Alliance for Human Rights v. City of Los Angeles*, Case No. 2:20-cv-02291-DOC, Doc. 39 (hearing on March 19, 2020, at 6:18–20); *see also* Joseph P. Charney, "Federal Judge David O. Carter Urges Los Angeles Politicians to End Litigation and Shelter the Homeless," *Medium*, April 12, 2020, https://medium.com/@josephcharney/federal-judge-david-o-bobca88773cd.

8   *L.A. All. for Human Rights*, No. 20-cv-02291-DOC-KES, Doc. 108, at 2, 4 (injunction and order dated May 15, 2020); *see also L.A. All. for Human Rights v. City of Los Angeles*, No. 20-cv-02291-DOC-KES, 2020 WL 2615741, at *5 (C.D. Cal. May 22, 2020), *vacated as a result of stipulation*, No. 20-cv-02291-DOC-KES, 2020 WL 3421782 (C.D. Cal. June 18, 2020).

9   *Mitchell v. City of Los Angeles*, Case No. 2:16-cv-1750-SJO-JPR (C.D. Cal.), Doc. 51 (Apr. 13, 2016) (minute order) ("important public health duty"); Doc. 119 (May 31, 2019) (settlement at pp. 7–15). Parts of the settlement are nonsensical. For instance, of the list of seizable property, Los Angeles agreed that it would only summarily destroy property posing an "immediate threat to public health or safety." Everything else must be kept in a storage facility, for months, where individuals can go to retrieve it. But what about evidence of a crime or contraband? The settlement, read literally, would seem to suggest that Los Angeles consented to store heroin or evidence of rape, at public expense, until its "owners" come back for it.

10 Jenna Chandler, "Homeless Advocates Challenge Constitutionality of Sweeps, Seizures," *Curbed Los Angeles*, July 19, 2019, https://la.curbed.com/2019/7/18/20699345/homeless-camps-seizures-lawsuit-constitutional.

11 Benjamin Oreskes, "L.A. Announced More 'Sensitive' Cleanups for Homeless Camps. Now It's Taking a Harder Line," *Los Angeles Times*, January 21, 2020, https://www.latimes.com/california/story/2020-01-21/los-angeles-homeless-encampment-cleanups.

12 *Garcia v. City of Los Angeles*, No. 19-cv-06182-DSF-PLA, Doc. 58 (Apr. 13, 2020).

13 Emily Alpert Reyes, "L.A. Council Votes to Resume Major Cleanups Near Shelters," *Los Angeles Times*, July 29, 2020, https://www.latimes.com/california/story/2020-07-29/la-to-resume-major-cleanups-near-shelters-critics-say-it-puts-homeless-people-at-risk.

14 *Joyce v. City & Cty. of San Francisco*, 846 F. Supp. 843, 845 (N.D. Cal. 1994). The argument of the *Joyce* plaintiffs had already been made by activists. See Harry Simon, "Towns Without Pity: A Constitutional and Historical Analysis of Official Efforts to Drive Homeless Persons from American Cities," *Tulane Law Review* 66, No. 4 (1992),660 ("Homeless arrest campaigns for sleeping in public and camping on public lands are also subject to constitutional challenge under the Eighth Amendment. Insofar as such arrests subject homeless persons to criminal liability for conduct they cannot avoid, arrests and convictions for sleeping in public may constitute cruel and unusual punishment.").

Notes

15 *Jones v. City of Los Angeles*, No. CV 03-1142 ER, 2004 WL 7321250, at *1 (C.D. Cal. Jan. 27, 2004), *rev'd and remanded*, 444 F. 3d 1118 (9th Cir. 2006), *vacated*, 505 F. 3d 1006 (9th Cir. 2007).

16 *Lehr v. City of Sacramento*, 624 F. Supp. 2d 1218, 1231 (E.D. Cal. 2009).

17 *Lehr*, 624 F. Supp. 2d at 1234.

18 *Veterans for Peace Greater Seattle, Chapter 92 v. City of Seattle*, No. 09-cv-1032-RSM, 2009 WL 2243796, at *1 (facts); *6 ("does not apply") (W.D. Wash. July 24, 2009). In addition to the cases above, below, *see also Betancourt v. Giuliani*, No. 97-cv-6748-JSM, 2000 WL 1877071, at *5 (S.D.N.Y. Dec. 26, 2000), *aff'd sub nom. Betancourt v. Bloomberg*, 448 F. 3d 547 (2d Cir. 2006) ("Plaintiff also argues that his arrest was a violation of the Eighth Amendment's prohibition against cruel and unusual punishment because he was arrested for sleeping in a public space. This claim must fail because an Eighth Amendment violation can only occur where a convicted person is involved").

19 *Martin v. City of Boise*, 920 F. 3d 584, 589 (9th Cir. 2019) (Berzon, J., concurring in the denial of rehearing en banc).

20 See, e.g., Lisa Halverstadt, "Months of Emails, Then a Mad Scramble: How the Hepatitis A Crisis Unfolded Behind the Scenes," *Voice of San Diego*, September 25, 2017, https://www.voiceofsandiego.org/topics/government/months-of-emails-then-a-mad-scramble-how-the-hepatitis-a-crisis-unfolded-behind-the-scenes (on San Diego's Hepatitis A outbreak).

21 Case 1:09-cv-00540-REB, Doc. 1 [original complaint Oct. 22, 2009]; Doc. 78 (Sept. 30, 2010), at 9–10. Similar objections have been raised in cases bringing this challenge. In *Joyce*, 846 F. Supp. at 845, a plaintiff said simply he didn't wish to burden his daughter by staying with her, despite her offer of a room. Is that shelter that is practically available? Or in *Lehr*, 624 F. Supp. 2d at 1221, a plaintiff refused shelter because that plaintiff felt unsafe there. Is that shelter practically available? In *Jones*, 444 F. 3d 1118, two plaintiffs were cited when they missed a bus to shelter and had to sleep on the street instead. For great analysis of the practical problems posed by *Martin*, see the briefs filed in support of Boise's certiorari petition before the US Supreme Court, including that of 33 California counties (https://www.supremecourt.gov/DocketPDF/19/19-247/116886/20190924165618585_19-247acCaliforniaStateAssociationOfCounties.pdf); the League of Oregon Cities (https://www.supremecourt.gov/DocketPDF/19/19-247/116935/20190925105749950_League%20of%20Oregon%20Cities%20Brief%20in%20Support%20of%20Petitioner.pdf); the International Municipal Lawyers Association (https://www.supremecourt.gov/DocketPDF/19/19-247/117067/20190925154526776_19-247%20Amici%20Brief%20IMLA.pdf); scholar Stephen Eide (https://www.supremecourt.gov/DocketPDF/19/19-247/117002/20190925141429243_19-247acStephenEide.pdf); and seven cities in Orange County (https://www.supremecourt.gov/DocketPDF/19/19-247/116996/

20190925140134189_19-247%20tsac%20Seven%20Cities%20in%20 Orange%20County.pdf).

22 Deon Joseph, "Hating the Fallout, Not the Homeless," *Medium*, June 15, 2019, https://medium.com/@deonjoseph/hating-the-fallout-not-the-homeless-c4140ebba066.

23 PBS NewsHour, "High Rents Force Some Silicon Valley to Live in Vehicles," YouTube, August 20, 2016, https://www.youtube.com/watch?v= KGo_KiM9Mv8.

24 Center for Health Impact Evaluation, "Recent Trends in Mortality Rates and Causes of Death Among People Experiencing Homeless in Los Angeles County," County of Los Angeles, Department of Public Health, October 2019, http://www.publichealth.lacounty.gov/chie/reports/HomelessMortality_ CHIEBrief_Final.pdf, at 3 (death rate), 5 (overdose rate and causes of death).

25 Case 1:09-cv-00540-REB, Doc. 77-1 (filed Sept. 30, 2010), at 6–7.

26 Reno City Attorney, Presentation to the Reno City Council & Redevelopment Agency Board, July 24, 2019.

27 Phil Matier, "Cleaning Up SF's Tenderloin Costs a Lot of Money – Soon It Might Cost Even More," *San Francisco Chronicle*, May 1, 2019, https://www. sfchronicle.com/bayarea/philmatier/article/Cleaning-up-SF-s-Tenderloin-costs-a-lot-of-13808447.php; see also Elijah Chiland, "LA Sanitation Needs $17M to Keep Up with Homeless Encampments," Curbed Los Angeles, February 22, 2018, https://la.curbed.com/2018/2/22/17040682/ homeless-encampments-los-angeles-cleanup.

28 Alexandra Yoon-Hendricks, "They Were Sacramento County's 250 Costliest, Most Vulnerable Homeless. A New Effort Is Helping," *Sacramento Bee*, January 5, 2019, https://www.sacbee.com/news/local/homeless/article 224778350.html

29 Nathan Heller, "A Window Onto an American Nightmare," *New Yorker*, May 25, 2020, https://www.newyorker.com/magazine/2020/06/01/a-window-onto-an-american-nightmare.

30 Janelle Bitker, "Mid-Market Restaurants Sue San Francisco over Homeless Encampments, Alleging Negligence," *San Francisco Chronicle*, July 17, 2020, https://www.sfchronicle.com/food/article/Mid-Market-restaurants-sue-San-Francisco-over-15416621.php; Janelle Bitker, "June Gloom, Dirty Streets Limit SF Restaurants' Outdoor Dining Options," *San Francisco Chronicle*, June 11, 2020, https://www.sfchronicle.com/restaurants/article/June-gloom-dirty-streets-limit-San-Francisco-15331222.php; Janelle Bitker, "SF Restaurant Turns to Dome Dining Amid Growing Homelessness on Streets," *San Francisco Chronicle*, August 6, 2020, https://www.sfchronicle.com/food/article/ Homelessness-crisis-leads-San-Francisco-15464909.php.

31 "Encampment Ordinance Goes Into Effect," LasVegasNevada.gov, October 19, 2019, https://www.lasvegasnevada.gov/News/Blog/Detail/ city-council-to-hear-first-reading-of-new-ordinance-designed-to-connect-

homeless-with-services-and-off-the-streets; see also Kate Cagle, "Crime Rate Among Homeless Skyrockets in Los Angeles," Spectrum News 1, May 7, 2019, https://spectrumnews1.com/ca/la-west/news/2019/05/07/crime-among-the-homeless-explodes-in-los-angeles (Serious crimes against homeless persons in Los Angeles rose dramatically between 2017 and 2018 – robbery was up 89%, larceny was up 86%, and rape was up 71%.).

32 Philip J. Cook, "Assessing Urban Crime and Its Control: An Overview," NBER Working Paper No. w13781, February 2008, https://ssrn.com/abstract=1091416.

CHAPTER 10

1   Doug Wyllie, "The Homeless Crisis: Why Service Providers Should Partner with Police," *Police Magazine*, July 27, 2018.

2   Wyllie, "The Homeless Crisis."

3   "Fargo Homeless Providers Partner with Police," Substance Abuse and Mental Health Services Administration, US Department of Health and Human Services, April 19, 2016, https://www.samhsa.gov/homelessness-programs-resources/hpr-resources/homeless-providers-partner-police.

4   City of Santa Rosa, Homelessness Solutions, https://srcity.org/2485/Homelessness-Solutions, accessed January 2019.

5   Kelli Kuykendall, email message to author, January 25, 2019.

6   "Council Takes Historic Vote to Address Homeless with New Bridge Shelter at Lighthouse Church," City of Costa Mesa News, January 16, 2019.

7   Faith E. Pinho, "As Costa Mesa Homeless Shelter Marks Its First Six Months, City Says 18 People Have Been Housed So Far," *Los Angeles Times*, September 26, 2019.

8   Pat Walsh and Al Venegas, eds., *California Police Chiefs Association: Homeless and Mentally Ill Work Group*, https://cebcp.org/wp-content/halloffame/Homeless-Working-Group-Report.pdf.

9   Andrew Brown, "San Diego Homeless Tent Shelters to Stay Open Through June," KPBS, September 18, 2018.

10 Aria Bendix, "San Francisco Spent $54 Million This Year on Street Cleanup – Here's Why It's Shelling Out Way More Than Other Cities," *Business Insider*, September 12, 2018.

11 Matier, "Little Bang for the Buck."

12 Mac Taylor, "Perspectives on Helping Low-Income Californians Afford Housing," California Legislative Analyst's Office, February 9, 2016.

13 "Addressing Homelessness Through the Private Sector," Mindy Nakamura, University of Tennessee, April 7, 2011, https://trace.tennessee.edu/cgi/viewcontent.cgi?article=2395&context=utk_chanhonoproj.

14 US Interagency Council on Homelessness, *Opening Doors: Federal Strategic Plan to Prevent and End Homelessness*, President Barack Obama, 2010, https://www.usich.gov/resources/uploads/asset_library/Opening%20

Doors%202010%20FINAL%20FSP%20Prevent%20End%20Homeless.pdf.

15 Andy Helmer, "Homelessness Requires a Private Sector Solution," *Tennessean*, November 15, 2017.

16 Helmer, "Homelessness Requires a Private Sector Solution."

17 Bethany Hines, "Nonprofit Helps Provide Jobs, Housing for the Homeless," CNN, June 25, 2018.

18 "Odessa," Shelters to Shutters, http://shelterstoshutters.org/story/odessa.

19 Mindy Nakamura, "Addressing Homelessness Through the Private Sector" (thesis, University of Tennessee, April 7, 2011).

20 Nakamura, "Addressing Homelessness Through the Private Sector."

21 Nakamura, "Addressing Homelessness Through the Private Sector."

22 Christopher F. Rufo, correspondence with the authors.

23 E. Fuller Torrey, "Homeless Mentally Ill Facts and Figures," Mental Illness Policy Org, https://mentalillnesspolicy.org/consequences/homeless-mentally-ill.html.

24 Rountree, Hess, and Lyke, "Health Conditions Among Unsheltered Adults in the U.S."

25 Rufo, correspondence.

26 Jutta Bolt, Marcel Timmer, and Jan Luiten van Zanden, "GDP per capita Since 1820," in *How Was Life? Global Well-Being Since 1820*, ed. Jan Luiten van Zanden, Joerg Baten, Marco Mira d'Ercole, Auke Rijpma, and Marcel P. Timmer (OECD, 2014), 57–72.

27 Howard Husock, "Opinion: Modern 'Asylums' Would Be a Compassionate Answer for Mentally Ill Homeless People," *Los Angeles Times*, November 11, 2019.

28 Husock, "Opinion: Modern 'Asylums.'"

29 Stephen Eide, "Same Old Homelessness Policy," *City Journal*, March 2, 2017, https://www.city-journal.org/html/same-old-homelessness-policy-15038.html.

CHAPTER 11

1 See, in addition to the discussion in chapter 3 above, Kusmer, *Down & Out*, 234.

2 On the deterrent effect of quality of life laws, see Andrew Golub, Bruce D. Johnson, Angela Taylor, and John Eterno, "Quality-of-Life Policing: Do Offenders Get the Message?," *Policing: An International Journal* 26, no. 4 (2003): 690–707, https://doi.org/10.1108/13639510310503578.

3 *Streetwatch v. Nat'l R.R. Passenger Corp.*, 875 F. Supp. 1055, 1057, 1066 (S.D. N.Y. 1995).

4 "Homeless a Growing Problem for SFPD at SFO," ABC7 News, May 21, 2019, https://abc7news.com/5311643.

5 *Rodgers v. Bryant*, 942 F. 3d 451, 453–54 (conduct covered), 456 (conduct not covered); *see also Loper v. New York City Police Dep't*, 999 F. 2d 699, 705

Notes

(2d Cir. 1993) (prohibition on begging in New York City allowed "certain religious, educational and fraternal organizations" to solicit contributions, but not the homeless).

6   But for a searching criticism of policies that "recast aggressive enforcement as a benevolent intervention," see Forrest Stuart, *Down, Out and Under Arrest: Policing and Everyday Life in Skid Row* (Chicago: University of Chicago Press, 2016), 5 (littering ticket to urge shelter attendance), 67 (jaywalking and obstruction of sidewalk tickets to urge shelter attendance), 92 ("recast"), 117 (targeting enforcement against those seen as needing services).

7   See generally Mark A.R. Kleiman, *When Brute Force Fails: How to Have Less Crime and Less Punishment* (Princeton, NJ: Princeton University Press, 2009), 34–41 (describing Hawai'i's HOPE program). And cities should be on guard against unjust and unintended collateral consequences of enforcement. Stuart, *Down, Out and Under Arrest*, 19 (suggesting that arrests or tickets led to loss of housing, loss of access to social services, or loss of employment).

8   *Tobe v. City of Santa Ana*, 9 Cal. 4th 1069, 1082 (facts), 1092 (disturbing nature), 1109 (duty) (1995). For other California cases, *see People v. Davenport*, 176 Cal. App. 3d Supp. 10, 15 (App. Dep't Super Ct. 1985) ("government can constitutionally prohibit overnight sleeping in public areas as part of its broad police powers"), *disapproved of by Tobe v. City of Santa Ana*, 27 Cal. Rptr. 2d 386 (Ct. App. 1994).

9   Heather Knight, "What Does London Lack That SF Has in Abundance? Misery on the Streets," *San Francisco Chronicle*, July 9, 2019, https://www.sfchronicle.com/bayarea/heatherknight/article/What-does-London-lack-that-SF-has-in-abundance-14080526.php.

10 See Michele Sviridoff, David B. Rottman, Brian Ostrom, and Richard Curtis, *Dispensing Justice Locally: The Implementation and Effects of the Midtown Community Court* (New York: Routledge, 2000), 1–10.

11 "Midtown Community Court," Center for Court Innovation, https://www.courtinnovation.org/programs/midtown-community-court.

12 "Community Justice Center," Superior Court of California, https://www.sfsuperiorcourt.org/divisions/collaborative/community-justice.

13 Randy Boggs, "San Francisco County Justice Center," YouTube, March 6, 2014, https://www.youtube.com/watch?v=0c6jqNvUQvA&feature=youtu.be.

14 Heather Knight, "5 Years In, Verdict Is Positive for S.F. Community Court," *SF Gate*, March 5, 2014, https://www.sfgate.com/bayarea/article/5-years-in-verdict-is-positive-for-S-F-5289195.php.

15 Yoon-Hendricks, "Sacramento County's 250 Costliest."

16 Alexandra Yoon-Hendricks, "This Man Cost Sacramento County More in One Year Than Any Other Homeless Person," *Sacramento Bee*, July 8, 2018, https://www.sacbee.com/news/article213820554.html.

17 Ken Furlong, Jessica Flood, and Brian Burriss, "Northern Nevada Regional Mobile Outreach Safety Teams," Presentation to the Nevada Legislature,

March 19, 2018, https://www.leg.state.nv.us/App/InterimCommittee/REL/Document/11266; "Mobile Outreach Safety Team (MOST)," Washoe County, NV, Human Services Agency, https://www.washoecounty.us/hsa/adult_services/most/index.php (Reno MOST program); "Forensic Assessment Services Triage Team (FASTT)," Nevada Legislature, February 5, 2014, https://www.leg.state.nv.us/App/InterimCommittee/REL/Document/5826?rewrote=1.

18 Taylor Pettaway, "Carson City's MOST Program Helps Those Dealing with Some Form of Mental Illness," *Nevada Appeal*, April 6, 2016, https://www.nevadaappeal.com/news/crime/carson-citys-most-program-helps-those-dealing-with-some-form-of-mental-illness.

19 Anita Chabria, "Trump Wants California Cops to Evict Homeless People. They Don't Want That 'Dirty' Job," *Los Angeles Times*, February 6, 2020, https://www.latimes.com/homeless-housing/story/2020-02-06/homeless-police-trump-santa-rosa-clear-encampment.

20 San Francisco Police (@SFPD), "Our Crisis Intervention Team (CIT) members work tirelessly to ensure we improve our response to crises involving the mentally ill," Twitter, February 13, 2020, https://twitter.com/SFPD/status/1228106173292769280.

21 City of Reno News Release, "Reno Police Program Works to Keep Mentally Ill Citizens Out of Jail," *This Is Reno*, April 11, 2012, https://thisisreno.com/2012/04/reno-police-program-works-to-keep-mentally-ill-citizens-out-of-jail.

22 Anne Knowles, "Forum Covers How Carson City Treats Serious Mental Health Issues," *Nevada Appeal*, January 9, 2019, https://www.nevadaappeal.com/news/local/forum-covers-how-carson-city-treats-serious-mental-health-issues.

23 Kirstie Alley (@kirstiealley), "Was in San Fran in Starbucks. A drunk street guy ran in screaming (it was terrifying) he began grabbing sandwiches & anything he could steal & ran out," Twitter, November 16, 2019, https://twitter.com/kirstiealley/status/1195786274688372737?lang=en.

24 Nakaso, "Honolulu Police."

25 Dan Nakaso, "Honolulu Police and Local Residents Team Up to 'Take Back' Chinatown from Homeless," *Star Advertiser*, May 15, 2019, https://www.staradvertiser.com/2019/05/15/hawaii-news/chinatown-homeless-police-and-citizens-join-forces.

26 Ken Stone, "What Does SDPD Neighborhood Policing Division Do? Mission Detailed," *Times of San Diego*, April 9, 2018, https://timesofsandiego.com/life/2018/04/09/what-does-sdpd-neighborhood-policing-division-do-mission-detailed.

27 Stone, "SDPD Neighborhood Policing Division."

28 Kevin Faulconer, "How San Diego Cleaned Up Its Act – And Got Real on Homelessness," *Hoover Institution*, October 30, 2019, https://www.hoover.org/research/how-san-diego-cleaned-its-act-and-got-real-homelessness.

Notes

29   Ben Westhoff, *Fentanyl, Inc.: How Rogue Chemists Are Creating the Deadliest Wave of the Opioid Epidemic* (New York: Atlantic Monthly Press, 2019), 1–10 (calling fentanyl responsible for the most destructive drug epidemic in American history; fentanyl lethal at two milligrams and can kill instantly; fentanyl has pushed drug overdose to the leading cause of death for Americans under 55 for first time in US history); Evan Sernoffsky and John King, "Fentanyl, Heroin Overdoses in San Francisco More than Doubled in 2019," *San Francisco Chronicle*, January 21, 2020, https://www.sfchronicle.com/ bayarea/article/Fentanyl-heroin-overdoses-in-San-Francisco-more-14993628.php.

30   Heather Knight, "Breed, Wiener Working to Ease Destructive Behavior on Street," *San Francisco Chronicle*, February 10, 2018, https://www.sfchronicle. com/news/article/Breed-Wiener-working-to-ease-destructive-12597752. php; see also Trisha Thadani, "Violent Assaults, Insufficient Care: Inside the Chaos of SF General's Emergency Room," *San Francisco Chronicle*, January 26, 2020, https://www.sfchronicle.com/politics/article/Violent-assaults-insufficient-care-Inside-the-15004548.php.

31   Heather Knight, "It's 'Life or Death': Recovering Addict Wants to Reinvent SF Response to Drug Crisis," *San Francisco Chronicle*, December 20, 2019, https://www.sfchronicle.com/bayarea/heatherknight/article/It-s-life-or-death-Recovering-addict-14920338.php.

32   "Governor Newsom Delivers State of the State Address on Homelessness," Office of Governor Gavin Newsom, February 19, 2020, https://www.gov. ca.gov/2020/02/19/governor-newsom-delivers-state-of-the-state-address-on-homelessness.

33   Lolita Lopez and Phil Drechsler, "Gangs of LA on Skid Row," NBC News, February 19, 2018, https://www.nbclosangeles.com/news/gangs-of-la-on-skid-row/167805; KOMO-Seattle, "Seattle Police Bust Drug Rings in Homeless Camps," May 15, 2019, https://komonews.com/news/local/seattle-police-bust-drug-rings-in-homeless-camps; Josh Harkinson and Prashanth Kamal-akanthan, "Inside the Nation's Largest Homeless Encampment," *Mother Jones*, YouTube, December 2, 2014, https://www.youtube.com/watch?v= pQn1z2HBlrA.

34   Theresa Walker, "Thousands of Pounds of Human Waste, Close to 14,000 Hypodermic Needles Cleaned Out from Santa Ana River Homeless Encampments," *Orange County Register*, March 9, 2018, https://www.ocregister. com/2018/03/08/thousands-of-pounds-of-human-waste-close-to-14000-hypodermic-needles-cleaned-out-from-santa-ana-river-homeless-encampments; Steve Large, "Debris from Homeless Camps Ending Up in Local Waterways After Storms," CBS Sacramento, January 9, 2018; Terry McSweeney, "Pollution Problem: Water District Pulls in San Jose, County to Help Clear Homeless Camps from Creeks," NBC Bay Area, February 9, 2016.

35   Joel Grover and Amy Corral, "Firefighters Lose Critical Tool to Battle Rise in Homeless Fires," NBC4 News, July 22, 2019; Amy Pollard, "Tent Fires Are on

the Rise Among the Homeless in L.A.'s Skid Row," *Slate*, July 24, 2018.

36   *See* Motion to Intervene, *Mitchell v. City of Los Angeles*, No. 16-CV-1750-SJO (C.D. Cal.), Doc. 120 (June 24, 2019).

37   Benjamin Oreskes, "Desperate to Get Rid of Homeless People, Some Are Using Prickly Plants, Fences, Barriers," *Los Angeles Times*, July 10, 2019.

38   *Butcher v. City of Marysville*, No. 2:18-CV-2765-JAM-CKD, 2019 WL 918203, at *1 (E.D. Cal. Feb. 25, 2019). *See also Shipp v. Schaaf*, No. 19-CV-01709-JST, 2019 WL 1644401, at *1 (N.D. Cal. Apr. 16, 2019); *Le Van Hung v. Schaaf*, No. 19-CV-01436-CRB, 2019 WL 1779584, at *1 (N.D. Cal. Apr. 23, 2019).

39   *Quintero v. City of Santa Cruz*, No. 5:19-CV-01898-EJD, 2019 WL 1924990, at *1 (N.D. Cal. Apr. 30, 2019).

40   Las Vegas Mun. Code 10.86 (Ord. No. 6710, § 1, 11-6-19). The text of the ordinance is available at https://www. lasvegasnevada. gov/News/Blog/Detail/city-councilto-hear-first-reading-of-new-ordinance-designed-to-connect-homeless-with-services-and-off-the-streets.

41   "Sanctioned Encampment Siting: Frequently Asked Questions," City of Seattle, https://www.seattle.gov/Documents/Departments/HumanServices/AboutUs/Encampment_Sites_FAQ_Matrix_Draft_DPD_Rule_10-6-15.pdf; Ketil Freeman, "Summary and Fiscal Note," Seattle Office of the County Clerk, http://seattle.legistar.com/View.ashx?M=F&ID=8001368&GUID=DA4CE604-39D1-445D-9639-005F84C9D70C.

42   Susie Steimle, "West Oakland Neighbors Shocked by City-Sanctioned Homeless Camp," CBS SF Bay Area, July 2, 2019, https://sanfrancisco.cbslocal.com/2019/07/02/w-oakland-neighbors-shocked-when-city-sanctioned-homeless-camp-moves-in; Sarah Ravani, "Oakland Proposes Crackdown on Homeless Campers in Parks and on Sidewalks," *San Francisco Chronicle*, December 4, 2019, https://www.sfchronicle.com/bayarea/article/Oakland-officials-propose-crackdown-on-homeless-14882712.php.

43   "City Opens 'Safe Parking' Lot for People Living in Their Cars, RVs," NBC San Diego, April 17, 2019, https://www.nbcsandiego.com/news/local/Safe-Parking-Program-New-Lot-Opens-Mission-Valley-508645261.html.

44   Andersen, "What Happened to SF's Controversial 'Sit-Lie' Ordinance?"

45   Trisha Thadani, "'We Don't Want to Be Outside': Homeless Say Few Beds Offered During Sweep Near Civic Center," *San Francisco Chronicle*, December 5, 2019, https://www.sfchronicle.com/bayarea/article/We-don-t-want-to-be-outside-Homeless-say-14882625.php#photo-18706717.

46   Susie Steimle, "Homeless Situation in San Francisco Union Square Goes from Bad to Worse," CBS SF Bay Area, November 28, 2017, https://sanfrancisco.cbslocal.com/2017/11/28/holiday-decorations-cant-hide-homeless-situation-in-san-francisco-union-square; *see also* Knight, "Breed, Wiener Working."

47   See, e.g., Bigad Shaban, Robert Campos, and Tony Rutanooshedech [sic], "San Francisco's $65 Million 'Street Cleaning' Budget Raises Concerns at City Hall," NBC Bay Area, April, 12, 2018, https://www.nbcbayarea.com/news/

local/san-franciscos-65-million-street-cleaning-budget-raises-concerns-at-city-hall; Keeling, "Major Medical Group Cancels."

48 See, e.g., Bigad Shaban, Robert Campos, Anthony Rutanashoodech, Mark Villarreal, and Jeremy Carroll, "Mayor Breed's First Year: Feces, Needles Complaints Decline; Trash Gripes, Homelessness Rise," NBC Bay Area, July 10, 2019, https://www.nbcbayarea.com/news/local/mayor-london-breed-first-year-in-office/154431.

49 Compare to Simon, "Towns Without Pity," 669 ("Official policymakers have openly stated their intentions to drive homeless individuals from cities.").

50 Heller, "A Window Onto an American Nightmare."

51 See "Richard Riordan Volunteers to Spend Night with Homeless," CBS Los Angeles, November 6, 2010, http://losangeles.cbslocal.com/2010/11/06/richard-riordan-volunteers-to-spend-night-with-homeless.

52 See, e.g., Heather Knight, "Beloved SF Homelessness Nonprofit Scales Back as 'Devastating' Crisis Takes Toll," *San Francisco Chronicle*, December 17, 2019, https://www.sfchronicle.com/bayarea/heatherknight/article/Beloved-SF-homelessness-nonprofit-scales-back-as-14911174.php.

53 Heather Knight, "The Tenderloin and SoMa: San Francisco's Safe Sites for Drug Dealers," *San Francisco Chronicle*, October 6, 2018, https://www.sfchronicle.com/bayarea/heatherknight/article/safe-sights-drug-dealers-tenderloin-sf-use-soma-13286197.php. The stories were collected by the *Chronicle* and caption the pictures accompanying the above article.

CHAPTER 12

1 Lee Romney, "S.F. Has a Plan for Homeless Problem," *Los Angeles Times*, July 1, 2004, https://www.latimes.com/archives/la-xpm-2004-jul-01-me-san-fran1-story.html.

2 "The Ten-Year Planning Process to End Chronic Homelessness in Your Community, a Step-by-Step Guide," US Interagency Council on Homelessness, accessed May 12, 2020, https://www.cdaid.org/files/municipal_services/USIGHomeless.pdf.

3 Joel John Roberts, "Did America's 10-Year Plan to End Homelessness Work?," *HuffPost*, April 2, 2012, https://www.huffpost.com/entry/did-americas-ten-year-pla_b_1394905.

4 Christopher F. Rufo, "The Moral Crisis of Skid Row," *City Journal*, January 11, 2020, https://www.city-journal.org/skid-row-los-angeles.

5 "The 2019 Annual Homeless Assessment Report (AHAR) to Congress, Part 1: Point-in-Time Estimates of Homelessness," n.d., 104.

6 "The State of Homelessness in America," Council of Economic Advisers, September 2019, 41, https://www.whitehouse.gov/wp-content/uploads/2019/09/The-State-of-Homelessness-in-America.pdf.

7 "The State of Homelessness in America."

8 Christopher F. Rufo is a contributing editor of *City Journal*. "Plot Twist," *City*

Journal, March 10, 2020, https://www.city-journal.org/progressive-narrative-on-homelessness.

9   "Neighboring Cities Are Pushing Homeless into L.A., Councilmen Alleged," *Los Angeles Times*, June 6, 2019, https://www.latimes.com/local/lanow/la-me-los-angeles-homeless-neighboring-cities-sidewalk-lawsuit-20190605-story.html.

10 "Average Rent in Culver City & Rent Prices by Neighborhood," RENTCafé, accessed May 12, 2020, https://www.rentcafe.com/average-rent-market-trends/us/ca/culver-city.

11 "Readers React: Don't Blame Culver City for L.A.'s Inability to Deal with Homelessness," *Los Angeles Times*, June 9, 2019, https://www.latimes.com/opinion/readersreact/la-ol-le-culver-city-homeless-20190609-story.html.

12 "3437 – 2019 Greater Los Angeles Homeless Count Presentation," Los Angeles Homeless Services Authority, accessed May 12, 2020, https://www.lahsa.org/documents?id=3437-2019-greater-los-angeles-homeless-count-presentation.pdf.

13 "2019 San Francisco Homeless Count & Survey."

14 "6,686: A Civic Disgrace."

15 "City of Seattle 2016 Homeless Needs Assessment," Applied Survey Research, accessed May 12, 2020, https://assets.documentcloud.org/documents/3480319/City-of-Seattle-Homeless-Needs-Assessment-March.pdf.

16 "City of Seattle 2016 Homeless Needs Assessment."

17 Scott P. Lindsay, *System Failure: Report on Prolific Offenders in Seattle's Criminal Justice System*, February 2019, https://downtownseattle.org/files/advocacy/system-failure-prolific-offender-report-feb-2019.pdf; Scott P. Lindsay, *System Failure Part 2: Declines, Delays, and Dismissals – Why Most Seattle Misdemeanor Cases Never Get Resolved and the Impacts on Public Safety*, September 2019, https://downtownseattle.org/app/uploads/2019/09/System-Failure-Part-2-Declines-Delays-and-Dismissals-Sept-2019.pdf.

18 "Press Release: City Pursues Strategies for Homeless, Panhandlers," Office of the Mayor, March 2, 2017, https://www.houstontx.gov/mayor/press/strategies-for-homeless-panhandlers.html.

19 "Houston Leads the Nation in Reducing Homelessness," SEARCH Homeless Services, accessed May 12, 2020, http://www.searchhomeless.org/houston-leads-the-nation-in-reducing-homelessness.

20 "Average Temperatures for Large US Cities in January," Current Results, accessed May 12, 2020, https://www.currentresults.com/Weather/US/average-city-temperatures-in-january.php.

21 "What Are Other Places Doing Successfully?," CalMatters, accessed May 12, 2020, https://calmatters.org/explainer/96080/embed/f6c23e70-28dd-11ea-963d-8304ae9d247c.

22 Katherine Timpf, "Seattle-Area Councilman: Hosing Poop-Covered

Notes

Sidewalks Might Be Racially Insensitive," *National Review* (blog), July 12, 2017,https://www.nationalreview.com/2017/07/city-councilman-hosing-poop-covered-sidewalks-might-be-racially-insensitive; "People in Houston 'at Risk of Being Arrested Just Because They Are Homeless,'" *The Guardian*, December 29, 2017, https://www.theguardian.com/us-news/2017/dec/29/houston-homeless-aclu-texas-ordinance.

23 Christine Gerbode, "City: Don't Want Folks Living Under Your Local Overpass? Then Show Us Where to Put Them," Swamplot, March 3, 2017, http://swamplot.com/city-dont-want-folks-living-under-your-local-overpass-then-show-us-where-to-put-them/2017-03-03.

24 Jesse Graham, Jonathan Haidt, and Brian A. Nosek, "Liberals and Conservatives Rely on Different Sets of Moral Foundations," *Journal of Personality and Social Psychology* 96, No. 5 (2009): 1029–1046, https://doi.org/10.1037/a0015141.

25 Christopher F. Rufo, "Waging Social-Justice War on the Taxpayers' Dime, *City Journal*, December 19, 2019, https://www.manhattan-institute.org/waging-social-justice-war-on-the-taxpayers-dime.

INDEX

The letter *t* following a page number denotes a table.
The letter *f* denotes a figure.

Index

Index

Index

First American edition published in 2021 by Encounter Books,
an activity of Encounter for Culture and Education, Inc.,
a nonprofit, tax-exempt corporation.
Encounter Books website address: www.encounterbooks.com

Manufactured in the United States and printed on
acid-free paper. The paper used in this publication meets
the minimum requirements of ANSI/NISO Z39.48—1992
(R 1997) (*Permanence of Paper*).

FIRST AMERICAN EDITION

LIBRARY OF CONGRESS CATALOGING-IN-PUBLICATION DATA

Names: Jackson, Kerry, 1960- author. | Rufo, Christopher F., 1984- author. |
Tartakovsky, Joseph, 1981- author | Winegarden, Wayne, 1968- author.
Title: No way home : the crisis of homelessness and how to fix it with intelligence
and humanity / by Kerry Jackson, Christopher F. Rufo, Joseph Tartakovsky,
Wayne Winegarden.
Description: New York : Encounter Books, 2021. | Includes bibliographical
references and index. |
Identifiers: LCCN 2020037431 (print) | LCCN 2020037432 (ebook) |
ISBN 9781641771641 (hardcover) | ISBN 9781641771658 (ebook)
Subjects: LCSH: Homelessness—United States. | Housing—United States. |
Poor—Government policy—United States.
Classification: LCC HV4505.J33 2021 (print) | LCC HV4505 (ebook) |
DDC 362.5/920973—dc23
LC record available at https://lccn.loc.gov/2020037431
LC ebook record available at https://lccn.loc.gov/2020037432

A Note on the Type

No Way Home has been set in Jonathan Hoefler's Whitney types. Originally developed for the Whitney Museum of American Art in New York, the types have been carefully designed to serve a wide variety of uses, from printed texts to on-screen display to large-scale signage. Whatever the application, the types' open characters and ample x-height have been shaped to maximize legibility, while the elegant drawing give the letters a warmth and ease of reading that is often lacking in sans-serif types.

DESIGN & COMPOSITION BY CARL W. SCARBROUGH